U.S. National Security and the Intelligence Services

While there are books that cover national security, intelligence collection, intelligence analysis and various intelligence services, *U.S. National Security and the Intelligence Services* is the first, all-inclusive book to examine intelligence agencies as a direct function of national security. It serves as a comprehensive text for students and a resource for those in the intelligence profession and national security scholars.

The book offers an in-depth understanding of the important role that the intelligence services provide to the national security of a nation. It also includes information on the various types of intelligence, collection methods, tradecraft and intelligence analysis methods, as well as intelligence-related resources. Coverage provides an overview of what national security is and its relationship with intelligence services of the United States, its key allies and hostile nations.

Key Features:

- Identifies the various national security threats and details the numerous U.S. and key allied intelligence services that work and collaborate to mitigate such threats
- Reviews the types of intelligence – outlining intelligence collection methods and intelligence tradecraft
- Explores how to determine the value of the intelligence collected, explaining the various methods of intelligence analysis and optimal methods to present conclusions

The roles the various agencies in the intelligence services play are as vital as the intelligence collected, the means by which it's collected and the methodology in which it is disseminated and analyzed. *U.S. National Security and the Intelligence Services* provides a handy reference outlining the framework, and the processes, that comprise the U.S. intelligence apparatus.

U.S. National Security and the Intelligence Services

Daniel J. Benny

CRC Press
Taylor & Francis Group
Boca Raton London New York

CRC Press is an imprint of the
Taylor & Francis Group, an **informa** business

First edition published 2023
by CRC Press
6000 Broken Sound Parkway NW, Suite 300, Boca Raton, FL 33487-2742

and by CRC Press
4 Park Square, Milton Park, Abingdon, Oxon, OX14 4RN

CRC Press is an imprint of Taylor & Francis Group, LLC

ISBN: 978-1-032-21999-8 (hbk)
ISBN: 978-1-032-21998-1 (pbk)
ISBN: 978-1-003-27084-3 (ebk)

DOI: 10.4324/9781003270843

Typeset in Palatino LT Std
by codeMantra

CONTENTS

ACKNOWLEDGMENTS

Office of Naval Intelligence
United Network Command for Law and Enforcement

AUTHOR BIOGRAPHY

 **Dr. Daniel J. Benny** is a full-time tenured Associate Professor with Embry-Riddle Aeronautical University Worldwide Campus teaching courses in intelligence and national security. He is also a Licensed Private Investigator and Court-Qualified Security Expert. He served ten years as a Naval Intelligence Officer with duty assignments at the Office of Naval Intelligence, Naval Intelligence Command, Naval Investigative Service, Willow Grover Naval Air Station, Fleet Intelligence Training Center Pacific, Fleet Rapid Support Team and Central Intelligence Agency.

He holds a Doctor of Philosophy in Criminal Justice from Capella University, Master of Arts in Security Administration from Vermont College of Norwich University, Master of Arts in Homeland Security: Counter-Terrorism Studies from American Military University, Master of Arts in Intelligence: Intelligence Operations from American Military University, Master of Science in Maritime and Naval Studies from Maritime College State University of New York, Master of Arts in History: Military History from Southern New Hampshire University, Master of Aeronautical Science in Aviation Aerospace Management from Embry-Riddle Aeronautical University, Bachelor of Arts in Security Administration from Alvernia College, Associate of Arts in Commercial Security and Police Administration from Harrisburg Area Community College, Graduate Certificate from United States Naval War College, Graduate Certificate from United States Air Force's Air University Air War College.

Dr. Benny's professional certifications include Certified Protection Professional (CPP) and Professional Certified Investigator (PCI) from ASIS International, Certified International Investigator (CII) from Council of International Investigators, Certified Fraud Examiner (CFE) from Association of Certified Fraud Examiners, Personal Protection Specialist (PPS) from Executive Protection Institute, Certified Security Trainer (CST) from Academy of Security Educators and Trainers, Certified Maritime Security Professional (CMSP) from International Association of Maritime

Security Professionals, Certified in Security Supervision and Management (CSSM), Certified Protection Officer (CPO)and Certified Protection Officer Instructor (CPOI) from International Foundation for Protection Officers and Certified Institutional Protection Manager (CIPM) from International Foundation for Cultural Property Protection.

He has had the following books *The Complete Guide to Physical Security, General Aviation Security, Cultural Property Security, Industrial Espionage, Maritime Security, Private Investigation and Homeland Security, United States National Security and the Intelligence Services* published by CRC Press/Taylor & Frances Group and *United States Coast Guard Auxiliary and Homeland Security* published by Nova Science Publishers.

Dr. Benny can be contacted at drbennypi@comcast.net or 717 574-9273. www.bennypi.com.

Dedicated to my rescue kids.

Sherlock

Mollie

Abbey

Athena

Luan

Jagger

1

National Security and the Need for Intelligence

NATIONAL SECURITY

In order to protect a nation, it is important to understand the history of today's concept of national security and what national security actually means. The first concept of national security can be traced to the period of the Civil War in England and the Thirty Years' War in Europe. At the end of these conflicts and the establishment of the Peace of Westphalia in 1648, the concept that a nation-state had sovereign control of all aspects related to a nation success and survival became paramount. This included the nation's domestic issues such as internal security, politics, religious, educational and social concerns. It also included external security through the protection of the nation's borders and beyond with the interaction between other nation-states.

This view of what national security was denounced in 1795 by the philosopher Immanuel Kent. His view was that nation-states should accept a new world order by which they are subservient to the common good of all nations and international law. This was the foundation of the current liberal concept of a world government through an organization such as the United Nations by which nations give up much of their individual sovereignty for the good of all. This is not national security. A nation without borders and its own governmental foundation and laws will cease to be a sovereign nation.

DOI: 10.4324/9781003270843-1

1

The Continental Navy was established on October 13, 1775 as part of the Revolutionary War effort. After the Revolutionary War and the United States becoming a Sovern nation the country tried to be neutral related to world events but understood the need to protect its global interest. A Department of War was established in 1789 to support the national security of the new nation. On April 30, 1798 the Department of the Navy was established to project power and to protect the maritime interest of the Unites States. With the War of 1812 with Britain the United States Navy and Army were critical in the defense of the nation and winning the war against Britain. Later in the 1800s during the Napoleonic Wars in Europe the United States remained neutral. The United States did not want to take action to risk the national security of the nation. During that period in history the United States continued to seek peace with nations such as Britain and France by means of international commerce and trade rather than taking sides with the ongoing wars in Europe.

As the United States entered the 19th century its position in the world changed. This was due to the advances within the United State from the industrial revolution and the nation's military growth. With the global reach of the United States, the nation became involved in the global power struggles and was able to continue to project its power through the United States Navy. With the global reach of the United States the issue of a national security strategy for the protection of nation became a critical issue.

As the United States entered into World War II in 1941 it found itself with no national civilian intelligence agency to protect the national security of the nation. There was at the time the Office of Naval Intelligence that dealt with maritime intelligence issues. There was the United States Army G2 Intelligence Unit covering land-based military intelligence and the Federal Bureau of Investigation (FBI) that dealt with espionage and intelligence inside of the United States. President Roosevelt wanted to establish a foreign civilian intelligence service that could take the covert intelligence war to the enemy overseas. On June 13, 1942 the Office of Strategic Services was established. President Roosevelt named an intelligent and forward-thinking Director of the Office of Strategic Services, William J. Donovan.

William J. Donovan's vision was to recruit operatives for the Office of Strategic Services that were diverse in their experience, talents and intelligence. He also recruited women as operatives. The recruitment of women was not common at that time in history for any intelligence service.

The potential operatives were screened based on their personal history, education, experience and physical capabilities. The extensive screening resulted in the best possible individuals being selected to serve with the Office of Strategic Services. Over 13,000 operatives were employed by the intelligence service.

Another innovation established by William J. Donovan was the concept of strategic intelligence analysis. This included collection and analysis of intelligence looking at the big picture of the threats related to espionage, intelligence collection and covert operations. This new concept was a unique contribution by the United States to intelligence tradecraft. All of these innovations related to the creation of the Office of Strategic Services led to the success of that intelligence service.

The Office of Strategic Services conducted intelligence operations through its Special Operations Branch. That branch ran unconventional warfare and intelligence campaigns. The operatives also engaged in psychological warfare. The activity of the Special Operations Branch was primarily in Europe, but they also operated in Asia during World War II. The principal mission was to "set Europe ablaze." This included ambush attacks, assassinations and sabotage of the Nazi forces and their facilities. The goal was to weaken the enemy and support the advancing Allied military forces.

One of the many successful missions was when the operatives of the Office of Strategic Services developed the "Jedburg" teams. These teams parachuted into France in support of the Normandy invasion by the Allied Forces. There were 93 three-person teams as part of these operations with the mission to collect intelligence, spread disinformation and take part in sabotage. After the invasion the Office of Strategic Services teams also worked closely with the French Resistance forces by helping to train and support their members.

One of the historic aspects of the Office of Strategic Services is the fact that the service recruited woman as covert intelligence operatives behind enemy lines. One of the outstanding female operatives was Virginia Hall. Virginia Hall was born in Baltimore, Maryland. Seeking a career in the Diplomatic Service she ended up in Europe working for the Department of State as a clerk before World War II. She lost her leg in hunting accident that ended the hopes of a career with the United States Diplomatic Service. As the war broke out in June 1941 she went to London and obtained a position with British intelligence. She was sent to France to coordinate intelligence activity with the French Resistance and escaped capture by the Germans in a daring departure by way of Spain. For her service she was made a member of the "Order of the British Empire by order of King George VI."

In March 1944 she was recruited by the Office of Strategic Services and accepted a mission in German-occupied Europe as part of the Special Operations Branch. Because of her artificial leg she could not parachute into the occupied area. She traveled to Europe in a British patrol boat and made her way behind enemy lines by land.

She gathered intelligence in order to map and establish drop zones for supplies to be dropped to commandos on the ground. She arranged safe houses and assisted the Jedburg teams after the successful landing of the Allies at Normandy. For the remainder of the war, she gathered intelligence and trained several battalions of French Resistance members on how to carry out unconventional warfare. Based on her outstanding service General William J. Donovan awarded Virginia Hall a Distinguished Service Cross. This was the only Distinguished Service Cross awarded to a civilian woman during World War II.

The Office of Strategic Services left a legacy of innovative and successful service that was of value in the war effort. The Office of Strategic Services was able to place operatives behind enemy lines to gather intelligence and wage unconventional warfare. That activity hindered the enemy and provided the Allied Forces with valuable intelligence to carry out their military mission successfully.

The success of the Office of Strategic Services was due to the foresight of William J. Donovan and the operatives that he recruited and trained. The success was also due to the actions of the operatives who gave it all in carrying out their various dangerous missions. Many of the13,000 operatives paid the ultimate sacrifice, death in the hands of the enemy.

The Office of Strategic Services had an important influence on intelligence tradecraft with the innovation of strategic intelligence analysis and the intelligence collection methods that were developed. The Office of Strategic Services set the standard for future of American intelligence services after the war. Based on the innovations in recruitment and training of operative, the intelligence collection tradecraft and covert missions, when the war was over the United States, realized that it needed a civilian intelligence service to operate globally. There was a need for the collection of intelligence in support of the national security interest of the United States. Based on the standards set by the Office of Strategic Services after war had ended and the Cold War began the Central Intelligence Agency was established On September 18, 1947.

How effective were the covert intelligence operations of the Office of Strategic Services during World War II to the war effort? The professional research concluded that the Office of Strategic Services was a very effective intelligence service that did contribute to the war effort and beyond. The Office of Strategic Services set new standards in the organization of an intelligence service, the recruitment and training of operatives, especially the recruitment of women intelligence operatives. The Office of Strategic Services developed the concept of strategic intelligence analysis and the use of covert intelligence operations combined with unconventional warfare. The intelligence provided to the Allied Forces as well as the training and support given to the French Resistance disruption to the German war efforts in German-occupied Europe was a vital asset and contributed to the successful outcome of the war in Europe. The totality of the activity of the Office of Strategic Services led to the creation of the Central Intelligence Agency and future United States intelligence services. Based on these facts the Office of Strategic Services covert intelligence operations during World War II was indeed effective to the war effort.

With the events of World War I and World War II the national security of the United States was threaten. During those two conflicts there was little danger to the United State mainland. At the end of World War II with the expansion of the Soviet Union, the spread of Communism, the threat of nuclear war and the commencement of the Cold War with the Soviet Union, the threat to the United States homeland was a reality. The United States could no longer base its national security on oceans to protect the nation from enemy threats. The United States took steps to enhance the national security of the new nation.

NATIONAL SECURITY ACT OF 1947

On July 6, 1947 the National Security Act of 1947 became law. As stated in the act:

> An Act To promote the national security by providing for a Secretary of Defense; for a National Military Establishment; for a Department of the Army, a Department of the Navy, and a Department of the Air Force; and for the coordination of the activities of the National Military Establishment with other departments and agencies of the Government concerned with the national security.

In addition to the National Security Act additional important national security structures such as the creation of the Central Intelligence Agency, the

National Security Agency, and the National Security Council were established. To further reduce the risk to the national security of the United States and its allies in Europe from the threat of the Soviet Union the North Atlantic Treat was formed. The National Security Act of 1947 directed all of intelligence services and military of the United States along with the National Security Council to coordinate their activities to identify threats to the national security. The goal was to develop a strategy to counter such threats.

For a nation to have national security it must have the power and ability to defend itself from both internal and external threats that include espionage, cyber-attacks, weapons of mass destruction terrorism and threats from hostel nations. The power of the nation must include a stable political, economic and infrastructure system. There must also be strong emergences services, law enforcement, homeland security, cyber security and military apparatus to counter the numerous internal and external threats. An effective intelligence service is a requirement to support the latter.

While a nation such as the United States needs to be independent and look after its own interest that does not mean that the United States should be an isolationist nation. That would be dangerous. There needs to be mutual support with other allied nations as part of the global community to the benefit of the United States. This mutual support would include collective security, defense and intelligence operations working within the confines of international law. The bottom line is that national security of the United States must protect and be for the benefit of the United States above all other nations.

INTELLIGENCE

Intelligence is collected by the intelligence services of the United States in order to obtain critical information on hostile nations, terrorist organizations and any other perceived threats in order to protect the national security of the United States. Intelligence according to the Office of the Director of National Intelligence is:

> *Intelligence is information gathered within or outside the U.S. that involves threats to our nation, its people, property, or interests; development, proliferation, or use of weapons of mass destruction; and any other matter bearing on the U.S. national or homeland security. Intelligence can provide insights not available elsewhere that warn of potential threats and opportunities, assess probable outcomes of proposed policy options, provide leadership profiles on foreign officials, and inform official travelers of counterintelligence and security threats.*

Intelligence collection is known as espionage. It has been stated that espionage is the world's second oldest profession. The collection of intelligence or practice of espionage is carried out by the intelligence services of the United States. Espionage is also conducted by its allied nations, hostile nations and terrorist organizations. The missions of the United States intelligent services are not only to collect intelligence but also to counter the collection of intelligence on the United States by allied nations, hostile nations and terrorist organizations. The threat of espionage against the United States continues to be a serious threat to the national security of the nation. *"Espionage is not a game; it's a struggle we must win if we are to protect our freedom and our way of life."* These words spoken by President Ronald Reagan during a November 30, 1985 radio speech have never been more relevant. In the world of national security, intelligence and espionage the war is never over (Figure 1.1).

According to the FBI espionage is:

> *(1) whoever knowingly performs targeting or acquisition of trade secrets to (2) knowingly benefit any foreign government, foreign instrumentality, or foreign agent. (Title18 U.S.C., Section 1831).* Trade Secrets and theft of trade secrets as:
>
> > *Trade secrets are all forms and types of financial, business, scientific, technical, economic or engineering information, including patterns, plans, compilations, program devices, formulas, designs, prototypes, methods, techniques, processes, procedures, programs, or codes whether tangible or intangible, and whether or how stored, compiled, or memorialized physically, electronically, graphically, photographically or in writing, which the owner has taken reasonable measures to protect; and has an independent economic value. "Trade secrets" are commonly called classified proprietary information, economic policy information, trade information, proprietary technology, or critical technology. Theft of trade secrets occurs when someone (1) knowingly performs targeting or acquisition of trade secrets or intends to convert a trade secret to (2) knowingly benefit anyone other than the owner. Commonly referred to as Industrial Espionage.*

> (Title 18 U.S.C., SECTION 1832)

UNITED STATES ESPIONAGE ACTS OF 1917

United States Espionage Act of 1917 was passed in to law to protect the United States during a time of war and peace and to make it a criminal offense to pass on information with intent to interfere with the operation or success

Figure 1.1   From the collection of Dr. Benny – a bust and 1984 letter to the author from President Ronald Reagan (photograph by Dr. Daniel J. Benny).

of the armed forces of the United States or aid the enemies of the United States. Theses offenses were punishable by death or by imprisonment for not more than 30 years or both. Under the United Espionage Act of 1917 it is also an offense to convey false reports or false statements with intent to interfere with the operation or success of the military or naval forces of the United States. This also included the promotion of enemies of the United States when the country is at war and to cause or attempt to cause insubordination, disloyalty, mutiny, refusal of duty, in the military or naval forces of the United States, or to willfully obstruct the recruiting or enlistment service of the United States. These offenses were punishable by a maximum fine of $10,000 or by imprisonment for not more than 20 years or both.

While the Espionage Act of 1917 dealt with espionage and subversion against the United States it did little to provide for the prevention and prosecution of individual taking part in industrial espionage against private industry (see Appendix A).

UNITED STATES ECONOMIC ESPIONAGE ACT OF 1996

The United States Economic Espionage Act of 1996 was passed in to law to provide for the prosecution of individuals taking part in industrial or economic espionage and the theft of trade secrets where it would benefit any foreign government, foreign instrumentally or foreign agent. The law specifically addresses Trade Secrets.

An important aspect of the Economic Espionage Act of 1996 was that it not only allowed for the prosecution of the perpetrators but also allowed the targeted company to seek financial reimbursement for loses to the organization as a direct result of the theft of trade secrets. This aspect of the law also holds the organization that facilitated or would have gained from the industrial espionage and trade secrets stolen from the targeted company (see Appendix B).

UNIFORMED TRADE SECRETS ACT

The federal espionage laws deal with the protection of United States government interest. And espionage perpetrated by foreign government, business and agents. To resolve this situation the Uniform Trade Secrets Act, published by the Uniform Law Commission in 1979 and later amended in 1985, has the goal of providing a uniform act as a legal framework for trade secrets protection for the private industry within the United States of America. The Uniform Trade Secrets Act aimed to codify standards and remedies regarding misappropriation of trade secrets that had emerged in common law on a state-to-state basis (see Appendix C).

HOMELAND SECURITY ACT OF 2002

After the devastating attacks of September 11, 2001 in 2002 the Homeland Security Act was passed. The goal of the Homeland Security Act was to bring all homeland security federal agencies under the umbrella of the new Department Homeland Security so that they could better respond to threats to the homeland of the United States through effective communications, intelligence collection and sharing and joint operations.

The agencies under the Department of Homeland Security include: Cybersecurity Infrastructure Security Agency, U.S. Customs and Border Protection, U.S. Citizenship and Immigration Service, Federal emergence Management Agency, U.S. Coast Guard, U.S. Immigration and Customs Enforcement, U.S. Secret Service and Transportation Security Administration (see Appendix D).

INTELLIGENCE REFORM AND TERRORISM PREVENTION ACT OF 2004

Once again after the devastating attacks of September 11, 2001 in 2004 the Intelligence Reform and Terrorism Prevention Act of 2004 was passed. The objective of this Act was to coordinate all of the intelligence services of the United States under the new position Office of the Director of National Intelligence. This reorganization was to allow for coordination in the collection and dissemination of intelligence between the numerous intelligible services of the United States.

This was to increase effective communications and field operations between the various intelligence agencies. The intelligence services now under the Office of National Intelligence include: Central Intelligence Agency, Defense Intelligence Agency, National Security Agency, National Geospatial Intelligence Agency, National Reconnaissance Office, and the intelligence services of the Army, Navy, Matie Corps, Air Force and Space Force. It also includes intelligence services of Department of Energy's Office of Intelligence and Counter-Intelligence, Department of Homeland Security Office of Intelligence Analysis, the US. Coast Guard, the Federal Bureau of Investigations, Drug Enforcement Agency Office of National Security Intelligence, Department of State Bureau of Intelligence and Research and the Department of the Treasury's Office of Intelligence Analysis (see Appendix E).

Intelligence is critical to protection of the National Security and Homeland Security of the United States from hostile nations and terrorist organizations. In the past the intelligence services of the United States have performed admirably to protect the nation such during the Cuban Missile Crises, the locating and killing of the mastermind of 9/11

Osama bin Laden and the tracking and killing of Iranian General and terrorist Qusam Soleimani. Unfortunately, there is an historical record of intelligence failure by the United States intelligence services. The attack by the Imperial Empire of Japan on Pearl Harbor on December 7, 1941 and the terrorist attacks on the World Trade Center complex in New York City, New York the Pentagon in Washington DC and the destruction of Flight 93 at Shanksville, Pennsylvania on September 11, 2001. In order to provide effective and timely intelligence to the nation the intelligence service must focus on the threat from hostile nations and terrorist organizations.

SHARING INTELLIGENCE

Within the United States Intelligence Community, it is vital that intelligence be shared between intelligence agencies, state and local law enforcement based on a need to know for the advantage of the national security. According to the Office of the Director of National Intelligence information sharing between the Intelligence Community and law enforcement leads to more effective interagency collaboration and protection of the nation. Since 9/11 there has been effective legal communication utilizing the Terrorism Task Force and the Fusion Centers established throughout the United States to share information related to terrorism and other national security threats. These two platforms enhance effective communication between the Intelligence Community, the FBI, the Department of Defense, state and local law enforcement.

According to the FBI they can share information related to specific and non-specific threats. These threats may include hostel surveillance, elicitation and respective unusual activity. It also includes test of security, bomb and other hostel incidents.

There has been information presented that support this legal exchange of information. There was the October 26, 2002 *Uniting and Strengthening America by Providing Appropriate Tools Required to Intercept and Obstruct Terrorism Act* that is commonly identified as the Patriot Act. On November 18, 2002 the Foreign Intelligence Surveillance Court (FISA) issues a report that removed some of the real and perceived barriers that allowed information sharing between the FBI, the Intelligence Community and the Department of Defense. It also opened up communication to public law enforcement and corporate security for non-classified information.

In March 2005 the Department of Justice put forth the Intelligence Sharing Procedures for Foreign Intelligence Counterintelligence Investigations. This permitted the FBI to share intelligence. The FBI now issues Intelligence Information Reports, Intelligence Assessments and Intelligence Bulletins.

With the new legal changes there has been enhanced information sharing between the Intelligence Community, FBI, Department of Defense, state and local law enforcement and even corporate security. Over the past 20 years since the September 11, 2001 this exchange of critical information has been effective in order to protect the nation. Open communication between all of the above shareholders is critical in the team approach in providing national security for the ultimate shareholders, the American people.

Bureaucratic politics and organizational dynamics can create issues with intelligence sharing. Bureaucratic politics is a foreign policy decision-making and bargaining process between government leaders. These leaders are often of different political parties and attempt to position the issues in the best interest of their political view and in the best interest of their political party but not always in the best interest of the nation.

Organizational dynamics is the behavior of the organization with regard to how individuals of the organization interact with one another. It includes the interaction at all levels of the organization. It also includes how an organization interacts with other like organizations such as members of the Intelligence Community. The lack of intelligence sharing between the members of the Intelligent Community is an example of the negative aspect of organizational dynamics. Bureaucratic politics and organizational dynamic can indeed have a negative impact on the intelligence analysis process.

As an example there have been very disturbing situations impacting the Intelligence Community and intelligence analysis in a negative manner based on bureaucratic politics and organizational dynamic by the President Biden administration. One of these includes the pronouncement by President Biden that climate change is the number one national security threat to the United States. According to President Biden, not the People's Republic of China, not the Russian Federation, not the Democratic People Republic of Korea, not Iran and not terrorism by climate change is the number one national security threat. If there ever was a negative example of bureaucratic politics this is it. This is being pushed on the Intelligence Community to be considered in their analysis. It is not based on facts and logic but solely on a misguided political agenda.

NATIONAL SECURITY THREATS FROM HOSTILE NATIONS

Hostile nations are those countries that pose a serious military, political, religious, economic or terrorism threat to the United States. There are currently five major hostile nations that pose such a threat to the United States. Those nations include People's Republic of China, the Russia Federation, the People's Democratic Republic of Korea, the Islamic Republic of Iran and now the Islamic Emirate of Afghanistan. While the specific threat from each of those six nations vary, the threat from each singular nation is significant. The People's Republic of China, the Russia, Federation and the People's Democratic Republic of Korea are traditional hostile nations. The Islamic Republic of Iran and now the Islamic Emirate of Afghanistan are hostel terrorist nations.

PEOPLE'S REPUBLIC OF CHINA

The People's Republic of China is the current number one intelligence, military, economic and political threat to the United States. This is supported by FBI Director Christopher Wray who stated in 2021, *"The greatest long-term threat to our nation's information and intellectual property, as to our economic vitality, is the counterintelligence and economic espionage threat from China."* The People's Republic China's extensive intelligence operations against the United States have been utilized to obtain critical intelligence from military, national security, economic, intellectual and political targets within the United States.

The Communist government of the People's Republic of China is utilizing tactics that attempt to influence public opinion in the United States as well as lawmakers in the Senate, Congress and the Administrative Branch of the government. The goal is to gain favorable policies to aid the People's Republic of China. This is also being accomplished with the investment in American corporation to the determent of the United States. As the United States corporation Nike's CEO stated in June of 2021, *"Nike is a brand of China."*

Other tactic being utilized by the People's Republic of China includes predatory business practices, infiltration of American university to systematically steal intellectual property and cyber-attacks to steal information and/or hinder the operation of American corporations. For many years to the current time China has used espionage against the

United States to include targeting United States colleges and universities. These institutions are targeted due the fact that they are centers for research and allow free movement and exchange of ideas. This is an opportunity for China to obtain Trade Secrets and other research of vale to their nation. The information is obtained in part by Chinese Foreign Nationals attending universes in the United States and acting as spies on their own accord or due to threat to their family in China if they do not obtain intelligence.

China also provides funding to United States universities and uses that for espionage as indicated in the following:

> In January 2020, the FBI arrested the chair of Harvard University's chemistry and chemical biology department, Charles Lieber, with 'one count of making a materially false, fictitious and fraudulent statement.' He failed to disclose his lucrative, deliberately opaque, and secretive financial arrangement with China through a program called the 'Thousand Talents Plan.' Under the arrangement, Lieber performed undisclosed work for the Chinese government through Wuhan University of Technology (WUT). Lieber is far from alone. In recent months, the United States has arrested numerous people in academic positions who either failed to disclose work for the Chinese government or actually engaged in straightforward espionage.

"The Chinese counter-intelligence threat is more deep, more diverse, more vexing, more challenging, more comprehensive and more concerning than any counterintelligence threat that I can think of," FBI Director Christopher Wray testified at a Senate Intelligence Committee hearing in 2019. The People's Republic of China views the assault on the United States as a "whole-of-society approach."

With regard the People's Republic of China's military they are full speed ahead in becoming the world military super power. The People's Republic of China now has the largest naval forces globally with close to 360 submarines and surface combat ships. The People's Republic of China is the world's top shipbuilding nation based on tonnage. The People's Republic of China's People's Liberation Army is the largest standing army in the world with 3,355,000 military personnel.

The People's Republic of China has more than 1,205 ground launched ballistic missiles along with an integrated air defense system consisting of Russian made S-400 and S-300 surface to air systems. The People's Republic of China has a stock pile of over 200 nuclear weapons with a goal to double that quantity as their nuclear arsenal is modernized. The People's Republic of China has a massive air force with over 2,500 aircraft, it is the third largest in the world. The People's Republic of China is also making progress with its military space enterprise program.

The People's Republic of China has a global military presence and especially as it applies to its naval force projection and land-based military operations globally. Based on all of these factors the People's Republic of China is the number one threat to the national security of the United States.

RUSSIAN FEDERATION

The Russian Federation is the current number two intelligence, military, economic and political threat to the United States. The Russian Federation like the old Soviet Union is a serious intelligence threat to the United States. The Russian Federation continues to systematically attempt to steal intelligence, military, political and economic data through espionage and cyber-attacks. The Russian Federation has also used cyber-attacks against United States military, governmental and corporate targets to disrupt those operations within the United States.

The Russian Federation is a serious nuclear threat to the United States with over 1,300 strategic weapons on over 550 land-, air- and submarine-based intercontinental ballistic missiles. The Russian Federation has an air force of 125 bombers and 1, 188 fighters. The Russian Federation navy consists of 603 ships and a sizable standing army. The Russian Federation has a standing military force of 1,500,000.

Based on the above factors the Russian Federation is a clear and present danger and is the second most serious threat to the United States. This threat is related to that nation's espionage activity, their nuclear capability and over all military stature.

DEMOCRATIC PEOPLE'S REPUBLIC OF KOREA AKA NORTH KOREA

The Democratic People's Republic of Korea as a hostel nation poses several serious threats to the United States. These threats include espionage, cyber-attacks, support for terrorism and future nuclear weapons. It is believed that the Democratic People's Republic of Korea has over 60 nuclear weapons as part of their ballistic missile program.

The Democratic People's Republic of Korea has the world's fourth largest standing military force with over 1.2 million personnel. This is a serious threat to South Korea and the United States who would respond to such an attack on South Korea. The Democratic People's Republic of Korea air force only consists of 26 older aircraft. The Democratic People's Republic of Korea naval forces include 16 patrol boats. Neither the Democratic People's Republic of Korea air force nor naval force poses any significant threat to the United States.

ISLAMIC REPUBLIC OF IRAN

The Islamic Republic of Iran is a terrorist nation-state. The most serious threat to the United States from the Islamic Republic of Iran is that as a nation it exports and funds terrorism against the United States. That nation also poses a capable cyber threat against the United States.

The Islamic Republic of Iran military has a total force of around 600,000. This includes its army, air force/air defense and naval forces. The nation's primary military threat comes from its naval forces in the areas of the Persian Gulf, Strait of Hormuz, Gulf of Oman, Arabian Sea and the Red Sea where they have the capability of attacks on international shipping.

The Islamic Republic of Iran seeks to be a nuclear nation and is working toward that goal. A nuclear Islamic Republic of Iran would be the most serious future threat from that terrorist nation.

ISLAMIC EMIRATE OF AFGHANISTAN

At the writing of this book Afghanistan was turned off to the Taliban by the United States Biden Administration after the disastrous withdrawal from that nation. Afghanistan as the new Islamic Emirate of Afghanistan is now a terrorist nation equipment with United States military weapons, equipment and aircraft. The Islamic Emirate of Afghanistan has aligned itself with the People's Republic of China, the number one enemy nation of the United States.

The threat from the Islamic Emirate of Afghanistan is terrorism. The attacks of September 11, 2001 originated from Afghanistan and on the 20th anniversary of the attacks, Afghanistan is now more dangerous than ever and will export terrorism against the United States.

NATIONAL SECURITY THREATS FROM TERRORISM

Terrorism has been a national security threat to the United States for decades and will continue to be a threat into the future. The threat comes from international terrorist organizations as well as domestic terror groups within the United States. The primary threat is from Islamic terrorist groups both within and outside of the borders of the United States. Violent domestic groups include white supremacy groups such as the Kul Klux Klan and Proud Boy. Other violent domestic groups include the self-identified Marxist group Black Lives Matters and ANTIFA. The following is a list of the some of the significant terrorist acts against the United States within the nation and abroad.

September 16, 1920 Bolshevist anarchist using a TNT bomb in a horse-drawn wagon left on Wall Street exploded killing 35 people with hundreds injured. This was the first vehicle bomb.

January 24, 1975 the Puerto Rican national group also known as the FLAN set off a bomb at the France Tarver in New York City. The attack killed four individuals.

November 4, 1979 the United States embassy in Iran was seized by Iranian students with the backing of that terrorist nation and holding 66 hostages that lasted for 444 days. They were released on the day Ronald Reagan was inaugurated President of the United States.

Between 1982 and 1991 additional hostages were taken by Hezbollah in Lebanon. Many were executed, several died in captivity and other were released. American Terry Anderson was held by the terrorist for 2,454 days.

April 18, 1983 the United States embassy in Beirut, Lebanon was destroyed by means of a suicide car-bomb attack by the Islamic Jihad. A total of 63 people were killed, 17 being Americans.

October 23, 1983 the United States military facility at the Beirut airport was attacked by Shiite terrorist suicide bombers in a truck killing 241 marines. A second attack within minutes killed 58 French troops at a barracks in West Beirut.

December 12, 1983 a Shiite terrorist truck bomb exploded at the United States embassy in Kuwait City, Kuwait killing. A total of five individuals were killed and 80 were injuring.

September 20, 1984 the United States embassy annex in East Beirut, Lebanon was attacked using a truck bomb. The attack resulted in the killing of 24 individuals.

December 3, 1984 Kuwait Airways Flight 221 en route from Kuwait to Pakistan was hijacked to Tehran, Iran. During the hijacking two Americans were killed.

April 12, 1985 a restaurant frequented by United States military in Madrid, Spain was bombed. A total of 18 individuals were killed and 82 injured. June 14, 1985 Hezbollah terrorist hijacked TWA Flight 847 from Athens to Rome. During the 17-day ordeal a United States Navy diver was executed.

October 7, 1985 Libya terrorist hijacked the Achille Lauro an Italian cruise ship. A United States citizen was executed.

December 18, 1985 airports in Rome and Vienna were bombed by Libya terrorist. A total of 20 people were killed to include five Americans.

April 2, 1986 a bomb exploded on TWA flight 840 from Rome to Athens killing four Americans.

April 5, 1985 Libya bombed a disco in West Berlin, Germany killing two and injuring hundreds.

December 21, 1988 Libya bombed Pan-Am Boeing 747 from London to New York over Lockerbie, Scotland killing all 259 onboard and 11 individuals on the ground (Figure 1.2).

Figure 1.2 Remembrance of All Victims of the Lockerbie Disaster who died on December 21, 1988 in Lockerbie, Scotland (photography by Dr. Daniel J. Benny).

February 26, 1993 a truck bomb exploded in the underground garage of the World Trade Center in New York City by al-Qaeda killing six and injuring 1,040.

April 18, 1995 a truck bomb set of by Timothy McVeigh and Terry Nichols an antigovernment group killed 168 people to include 19 children at the federal office building in Oklahoma City, Oklahoma.

November 13, 1985 a car bomb killed five United States military members at the military headquarters in Riyadh, Saudi Arabia.

June 25, 1996 a truck bomb exploded in Saudi Arabia outside the Khobar Towers United States military complex killing 19 American military personnel and injuring hundreds. The attack was carried out by Hezbollah.

August 7, 1998 the United States embassies in Nairobi, and Kenya were attacked by al-Qaeda using truck bombs. Over 224 individuals were killed.

October 12, 2000 the USS Cole was struck with a watercraft bomb killing 19 sailors and causing damage to the ship. The attack was carried out by al-Qaeda.

September 11, 2001 aircraft were flown into the World Trade Center in New York City, New York, the Pentagon in Arlington, Virginia and a commercial aircraft crashed at Shanksville, Pennsylvania. The attack was carried out by al-Qaeda (Figure 1.3).

Figure 1.3   September 11, 2001 (photograph by Dr. Daniel J. Benny).

June 14, 2002 a bomb exploded outside the American Consulate in Karachi, Pakistan killing 12. Attack carried out by al-Qaeda.

May 12, 2003 al-Qaeda suicide bombers killed 34 at a housing compound for Westerners in Riyadh, Saudi Arabia.

June 11, 2004 terrorists kidnapped and executed Paul Johnson Jr and American in Riyadh, Saudi Arabia.

December 6, 2004 six United States consulate employees were killed in Jeddah, Saudi Arabia.

November 9, 2005 al-Qaeda succeed bombers attacked three American hotels in Amman, Jordan killing 57.

May 26, 2008 six United States service members were killed by a suicide bomber in Tarmiyah, Iraq.

November 26, 2008 five Americans were killed when hotels were attacked in India.

June 1, 2009 a Muslim convert Abdulhakim Muhammed was killed by military recruiters in Little Rock, Arkansas.

December 25, 2009 a Nigerian man attempted to ignite as explosive hidden in his underwear on a flight from Amsterdam to Detroit.

December 30, 2009 in Iraq a suicide bomber kills eight American civilians, seven of them CIA agents, at a base in Afghanistan. It's the deadliest attack on the agency since 9/11. The attacker is reportedly a double agent from Jordan who was acting on behalf of al-Qaeda.

May 1, 2010 a car bomb was discovered in Time Square New York City but was not ignited.

May 10, 2110 in Jacksonville, Florida: a pipe bomb exploded. Approximately 60 Muslims are praying in the mosque. The attack causes no injuries.

January 11, 2011 in Spokane, Washington: a pipe bomb is discovered along the route of the Martin Luther King, Jr. memorial march.

September 11, 2012 in Benghazi, Libya: militants armed with antiaircraft weapons and rocket-propelled grenades fire upon the American consulate, killing U.S. ambassador to Libya Christopher Stevens and three other embassy officials. A group closely linked to al-Qaeda orchestrated the attack.

April 14, 2013 in Boston, Massachusetts multiple bombs exploded near the finish line of the Boston Marathon. Three people were killed and 260 people were injured. The attack was carried out by Islamic followers Tamerlan Tsarnaev and Dzhokhar A. Tsarnaev from Russia.

August 19, 2014 ISIS behead American journalist James Foley, September 2, 2014 an ISIS militant decapitates American journalist, Steven Sotloff who worked for *Time* and other news outlets.

December 2, 2015 in San Bernardino, California 14 people are killed and more than 20 wounded when two people open fire at a holiday party at the Inland Regional Center. The attackers were Islamic husband and wife Syed Rizwan Farook and Tashfeen Malik.

June 12, 2016 a mass shooting at an Orlando nightclub leaves 50 people dead, including the gunman, and more than 50 injured. The shooter is identified as Omar Mateen who pledged his allegiance to ISIS via a 911 call from inside the nightclub. This massacre is the deadliest mass shooting on at the time.

October 31, 2017 a man drove his rented Home Depot truck near the World Trade Center in New York and plowed his vehicle into pedestrians along the West Side Highway bike path, killing eight and wounding another 11. He claimed that this attack was for ISIS.

Summer 2020 ANTIFA and Black Lives Matter rioted in numerous major cities across the United States causing deaths and serious property damage. It includes an attack on the White House in Washington, DC and several federal court houses across the United States.

January 6, 2021 rioters breach the United States Capitol in Washington, DC as part of a protest against the 2020 Presidential election.

REVIEW EXERCISE

The Attack on Pearl Harbor

On December 7, 1941 the Imperial Empire of Japan using aircraft from their naval forces attacked United States naval forces at Pearl Harbor, Hawaii. Conduct research and describe the intelligence failures of the United States that led up to the attack. Describe how intelligence could have been utilized by the United States that could have prevented the attack by the Imperial Empire of Japan. Describe why effective intelligence is vital to the national security of a nation. An excellent source to use for this exercise is to watch the Film *TORA TORA TORA*.

REFERENCES

9/11 Commission. 2004. *The 9/11 Commission Report*. New York: W.W. Norton & Company.

Allen, Thomas. 2008. *Declassified: 50 Documents That Changed History*. Washington, DC: National Geographic.

Best Jr., Richard. 2014. "Leadership of the U.S. Intelligence Community: From DCI to DNI," *International Journal of Intelligence and Counterintelligence* Volume 27, Issue 2. http://ezproxy.apus.edu/login?url=http://dx.doi.org/10.1080/08850607.2014.872533

Brown, Anthony. 1976. *The Secret War Report of the OSS.* New York: Berkley Publishing.

Central Intelligence Agency. 2000. *The Office of Strategic Service America's First Intelligence Agency.* Washington, DC: Central Intelligence Agency Public Affairs.

CIA. 2021. *CIA Factbook, Afghanistan.* Langley: CIA.

CIA. 2021. *CIA Factbook, China.* Langley: CIA.

CIA. 2021. *CIA Factbook, Iran.* Langley: CIA.

CIA. 2021. *CIA Factbook, North Korea.* Langley: CIA

CIA. 2021. *CIA Factbook, Russia.* Langley: CIA.

Cornell Law School. 2021. *Police Intelligence.*32 CFR § 637.17- Police Intelligence. | CFR | US Law | LII / Legal Information Institute (cornell.edu).

Cypher Brief. 2021. China Focuses Espionage on US College and Universities. Retrieved from China Focuses Espionage on U.S. Colleges and Universities (thecipherbrief.com).

DoD. 2020. *Military and Security Development Involving the Peoples Republic of China.* Washington, DC: Department of Defense.

Dulles, Allen. 1963. *The Craft of Intelligence.* New York: Harper & Row.

Dulles, Allen. 1968. *Great True Spy Stories.* Secaucus, NJ: Castle.

FBI. 2021. Enhancing Information Sharing Initiatives. FBI — Enhancing Information Sharing Initiatives.

FBI. 2021. *The Threat from China.* Retrieved from The China Threat — FBI.

Fugat, Kinicki. 2012. *Orgabizational Dynamics.* Mount Pleasant, MI: Central Michigan University.

Garbo, Cynthia. 1999. "Sisterhood of Spies: The Women of the OSS," *The Journal of Military History* Volume 63, Issue 1: 218–220.

Heaps, Jennifer. 1998. "Tracking Intelligence Information: The Office of Strategic Services," *The American Archivist* Volume 61, Issue 2: 287–308.

James, Sandy. 2017. "Donovan's Devils: OSS Commandos behind Enemy Lines-Europe, World War II," *The Journal of Military History* Volume 81, Issue 1: 227–232.

Jones, Christopher. 2010. *Bureaucratic Politics and Organizational Process Modes.* New York: Oxford Press.

Lenzenweger, Mark. 2015. "Factors Underlying the Psychological and Behavioral Characteristics of Office of Office of Strategic Services Candidates," *Journal of Personality Assessment* Volume 12, Issue 4: 100–110.

Lovell, Stanley. 1964. *Of Spies & Stratagems.* New York: Prentice Hall.

Mehta, Aron. 2921. *Climate Change is now ta National Security Procrit for the Pentagon.* Washington, DC: Defense News.

O' Donnell, Patrick. 2004. *Operatives, Spies and Saboteurs: The Untold Story of the Men and Women of World War II's OSS.* New York: Free Press.

Office of the Director of National Intelligence. (ODNI). 2013. *U.S. National Intelligence: An Overview.* Washington, DC: ODNI.

Office of the Director of National Intelligence. 2021. *Law Enforcement Information Sharing.* Law Enforcement Information Sharing (dni.gov).

Richelson, Jeffery. 2016. *The US Intelligence Community.* Boulder, CO: Westview Press.

Shaw, Eric. 2019. China Trying to Infiltrate US Colleges to Recruit Spies, Indoctrinate Students, Intelligence Agencies Say. Retrieved from China Trying to Infiltrate US Colleges to Recruit Spies, Indoctrinate Students, Intelligence Agencies Say | Fox New.

Stevenson, William. 1976. *A Man Called Intrepid: The Secret War.* New York: Ballantine Books.

Wells, Robert. 2010. "Secret Operations of the OSS," *The OSS Society Journal* Fall 2010. 27–30.

2

United States Intelligence Services

UNITED STATES NATIONAL INTELLIGENCE COMMUNITY

Office of the Director of National Intelligence

The Office of the Director of National Intelligence and the Director of National Intelligence was establish after the 9/11 attacks on the United States with the Intelligence Reform and Terrorism Act of 2004. This created a Cabinet-level intelligence position.

The Office of the Director of National Intelligence Director for National Intelligence serves as the head of the United States Intelligence Community. In this position the director oversees and directors the United States National Intelligence Program. The Director for National Intelligence is the principle to the President on intelligence issues. The Director for National Intelligence also advises the National Security Council and the Homeland Security Council on all intelligence matters. The Director for National Intelligence is appointed by the President and is confirmed by the Senate. The Office of the Director for National Intelligence is staffed by members of the Intelligence Community and focuses on the core mission of the National Intelligence Program. Prior to the establishment of the Office of the Director of National Intelligence the Director of the Central Intelligence Agency also served as the Director of National Intelligence.

DOI: 10.4324/9781003270843-2

Central Intelligence Agency

At the start of World War II, the United States did not have civilian intelligence service that could operate and collect intelligence outside of the nation. In 1941 the Office for Coordination of Information was established to begin to collect intelligence for the United States. In 1942 the name was changed to the Office of Strategic Services. The Office of Strategic Services operated throughout the war years overseas in the collection of intelligence. The Office of Strategic Services also conducted extensive covert operations behind enemy lines. At the end of World War II the Office of Strategic Services was disbanded, and the intelligence collection element of the United States was named the Strategic Service Unit.

With the onset of the Cold War and the threats from the Soviet Union as well as the threat from other hostile nations around the globe the mission of the organization was expanded, and in 1946 the organization was renamed the National Intelligence Authority with a working group known as the Central Intelligence Group. There was still a need for a professional civilian intelligence service, and with the passage of the National Security Act of 1947 that same year the Central Intelligence Agency was established. The Central Intelligence Agency became the principal intelligence service of the United States to collect foreign intelligence in the United Stated as long as United States citizens were not targeted. The Central Intelligence Agency was also authorized to collect intelligence globally for analysis through the use of technical collection methods, human intelligence and the use of covert operation.

The Central Intelligence Agency initially was located in Washington D.C. but later moved to Langley, Virginia, upon the completion of the new Central Intelligence Agency headquarters complex that was designed by Allen W. Dulles, the first civilian Director of the Central Intelligence Agency who served from 1952 until 1961. Historically Dulles is the most well known of the Directors in addition to George H. W. Bush and William Casey (Figure 2.1).

Today the mission of the Central Intelligence Agency is "At its core, our mission is to gather and share intelligence to protect our nation from threats. Our highest principles guide our vision and all that we do: integrity; service; excellence; courage; teamwork; and stewardship." This is accomplished through the collection of foreign intelligence that is vital to the protection of the United States, to produce objective all-source analysis of intelligence collected to the benefit of the nation, to conduct effective covert operations and actions as directed by the President of the United States and finally to safeguard the secrets that keep the United States safe.

Figure 2.1 From the collection of Dr. Benny, CIA official photograph of Allen W. Dulles, first civilian Director of the CIA, and his autograph.

National Security Agency

Before the establishment of the National Security Agency there was the Armed Forces Security Agency created on May 20, 1949 to collect signals intelligence (SIGINT). Contributing to the Armed Forces Security Agency were the Naval Security Group, the Army Security Agency and the Air Force Security Service. The drawback to this organization was that it was limited to Department of Defense intelligence issues. To resolve this issue and to create a civilian version of the agency on October 23, 1952 the National Security Agency was established. The National Security Agency headquarters is located on Fort George G. Mead in Maryland.

Today the primary mission of the National Security Agency is to collect, process, analyze, produce and then to disseminate SIGINT to the United States government. The National Security Agency is authorized to collect this intelligence by open-source methods or covert operations. The National Security Agency also has a responsibility to provide counterintelligence operations related to SIGINT as well as the development of regulations related to the security classification of SIGINT information.

Special Collection Service

The Special Collection Service headquarters is located in Beltsville, Maryland and is a joint operation between the Central Intelligence Agency and the National Security Agency. The Special Collection Service works in cover operations "black-bag jobs" and also the installation of intelligence communications antennas in nondescript locations to aid in intelligence collection.

National Geospatial Intelligence Agency

The National Geospatial Intelligence Agency was established on November 24, 2003 and its headquarters is located on Fort Belvoir, Virginia. The mission of the National Geospatial Intelligence Agency is to oversee all air-, satellite- and ground-based imagery and mapping related to intelligence collection, analysis, product and dissemination.

National Reconnaissance Agency

On September 6, 1961 the National Reconnaissance Agency was established. It was established as a joint Central Intelligence Agency, United States Air Force and United States Navy to facilitate imagery intelligence (IMINT) and SIGINT collection. The National Reconnaissance Agency is located in Chantilly, Virginia. Their missions today include support of intelligence communications, imagery and space launch.

National Underwater Reconnaissance Office

The National Underwater Reconnaissance Office was established in 1969 as a joint effort between the Central Intelligence Agency and the United States Navy. The National Underwater Reconnaissance Office serves as a platform to employ submarines for intelligence operations. This includes recovery of sunken submarines such as the Soviet K-29 submarine. The submarines are also used to target hostile nations' underwater communications lines, undersea mapping and the collect single's intelligence.

The submarines under National Underwater Reconnaissance Office are also used for special operations to insert Central Intelligence Agency and United States Navy Seal operative for special operations missions.

National Security Council

The National Security Council was created by the National Security Act of 1947. It was later amended by the National Security act of 1949. The National Security Council is utilized by the President of the United States as a forum in making decisions on national security, intelligence and foreign policy issues. Included as part of the National Security Council are the President's senior national security advisors and the cabinet officials.

UNITED STATES LAW ENFORCEMENT INTELLIGENCE COMMUNITY

Department of Justice Office of Intelligence

The mission of the Department of Justice Office of Intelligence is to prevent acts of terrorism and hostile foreign intelligence activities and operations against the United States. The National Security Division of the Department of Justice Office of Intelligence since the terror attacks of 9/11 has been tasked to conduct intelligence operations involving the Foreign Intelligence Act (see Appendix F). The Department of Justice Office of Intelligence also conducted oversight of intelligence activity.

Federal Bureau of Investigation

The Bureau of Investigation was established on July 26, 1908 and in 1935 named the Federal Bureau of Investigation. J. Edgar Hoover was the first Director of the Federal Bureau of Investigation and served in that position until his death on May 2, 1972 (Figure 2.2).

The Federal Bureau of Investigation is primary federal law enforcement agency for the United States related to criminal investigations. As it is related to intelligence according to the Federal Bureau of Investigation;

The FBI has been responsible for identifying and neutralizing ongoing national security threats from foreign intelligence services since 1917, nine years after the

Figure 2.2 From Dr. Benny's collection – a 1947-autographed photograph of J. Edgar Hoover, the first Director of the Federal Bureau of Investigation.

Bureau was created in 1908. The FBI's Counterintelligence Division, which is housed within the National Security Branch, has gone through a lot of changes over the years, and throughout the Cold War the division changed its name several times. But foiling and countering the efforts of the Soviet Union and other communist nations remained the primary mission.

The current mission of the Federal Bureau of Investigation encompasses much more and is the lead agency for the investigation and prevention of intelligence activities in the United States through its Counterintelligence Division. The goals of that Division are:

Protect the secrets of the U.S. Intelligence Community, using intelligence to focus investigative efforts, and collaborating with our government partners to reduce the risk of espionage and insider threats.

Protect the nation's critical assets, like our advanced technologies and sensitive information in the defense, intelligence, economic, financial, public health, and science and technology sectors.

Counter the activities of foreign spies. Through proactive investigations, the Bureau identifies who they are and stops what they're doing.
Keep weapons of mass destruction from falling into the wrong hands, and use intelligence to drive the FBI's investigative efforts to keep threats from becoming reality.

The Federal Bureau of Investigation continues to be the primary federal agency responsible for the investigation of espionage and intelligence issues within the United States. The Federal Bureau of Investigation works closely with other federal intelligence and law enforcement agencies as well as foreign counterparts to accomplish this mission. There is also excellent corporation with state and local law enforcement agencies in the United States.

Department of Homeland Security
Office of Intelligence Analysis

Only 11 days after the September 11, 2001, terrorist attacks on the United States, Pennsylvania Governor Tom Ridge was appointed as the first Director of the Office of Homeland Security. With the passage of the Homeland Security Act by Congress in November 2002, the Department of Homeland Security was officially established as Cabinet-level department to further coordinate and unify national homeland security efforts, opening its doors on March 1, 2003 (Figure 2.3).

Within the Department of Homeland Security is the Office of Intelligence Analysis. The Office of Intelligence Analysis is an exclusive member of the United States Intelligence Community. It is the only member of the Intelligence Community authorized by statute with delivering intelligence to state, local, tribal and territorial and private sector partners in the United States. The goal is to provide those intelligence partners with adequate intelligence related to threats against the United States to secure the homeland of the nation.

Department of State Bureau of Intelligence and Research

According to the Department of State the mission of the Department of State Bureaus of Intelligence and Research is to: *"The Bureau of Intelligence and Research's (INR) primary mission is to harness intelligence to serve U.S. diplomacy."* The bureau was established within the Department of State in 1947. The Bureaus of Intelligence and Research obtains all-source intelligence

Figure 2.3 Dr. Daniel J. Benny's Founding Member certificate from the Director of Homeland Security Tom Ridge, issued on March 1, 2003.

information in order to keep the United States foreign policy makers of intelligence information that would be critical to their decision-making.

The Department of State Bureaus of Intelligence and Research works closely with other United States intelligence agencies to keep current on intelligible matters affecting the Department of State and its mission. The Bureau also conducts intelligence analytical research and provides the results of the research to other members of the Intelligence Community.

Department of the Treasury Office of Intelligence Analysis

The Department of the Treasury Office of Intelligence Analysis has become a more significant intelligence service since the terrorist attacks of September 11, 2001. In 2004 the Department of the Treasury Office of Intelligence Analysis became an official member of the United States Intelligence Community. The primary mission of the Department of the Treasury Office of Intelligence Analysis is the tracking of financial transactions and money related to terrorism activity and espionage from enemy nations against the United States. This is accomplished by intelligence analysis of transactions and intelligence receded with regard to terrorism or espionage activity.

Department of Energy Office of Intelligence and Counterintelligence

The Department of Energy Office of Intelligence and Counter-Intelligence can be derived from the National Security Council Intelligence Directive No. 1 of 1947. The intelligence and counterintelligence mission of the Department of Energy Office of Intelligence and Counterintelligence is the protection of all United States nuclear assets from espionage, theft and sabotage. This includes United States nuclear weapons and stockpiles, nuclear testing facilities, nuclear power plants and nuclear waste storage facilities.

The mission of the Department of Energy Office of Intelligence and Counterintelligence also include the tracking of international nuclear arms globally. This is accomplished through intelligence collection and analysis. This information is utilized for United State foreign policy matters, support for military operations and homeland security operations to protect the United States.

Drug Enforcement Administration Office of National Security Intelligence

The mission of the Drug Enforcement Administration Office of National Security Intelligence operating under the Department of Justice intelligence is to provide strategic and operations intelligence globally for the agency in the effort to stop illegal drug trafficking and the protection of the United States. The Drug Enforcement Administration Office of National Security Intelligence works closely with other United States law enforcement agencies, intelligence agencies and the United States Coast Guard.

United States Secret Service Intelligence

The United States Secret Service was established in 1865 to stop the spread of counterfeit money from the southern states during the Civil War. With the assassination of President William McKinley in 1901

Congress requested Secret Service protection for the President which began full time in 1902. With the attempted assassination of President Harry Truman in 1951 Congress enacted a law authorizing the permanent protection of the President and Vice President of the United States by the Secret Service.

The United States Secret Service Intelligence has the mission of providing intelligence for the protection of the President of the United States at the White House and all other locations utilized by the President globally. This includes all travel itineraries by the President. The United States Secret Service is also responsible for the protection of high-profile individuals visiting the United States. This is accomplished through the 1998 creation of the Secret Service National Threat Assessment Center in Washington, D.C.

UNITED STATES MILITARY INTELLIGENCE COMMUNITY

Defense Intelligence Agency

In August 1961 the Defense Intelligence Agency was established. The mission of the Defense Intelligence Agency was to consolidate all military intelligence arising from the various military intelligence organizations. The Defense Intelligence Agency headquarters is located at Bolling Air Force Base in Washington, D.C. The Defense Intelligence Agency operates the Human Intelligence and Counter Intelligence Center and Defense Intelligence Operations and Coordination Center. Defense Intelligence Agency also conducts research related to military intelligence projects and the development of new intelligence equipment and operational platforms. The agency also advises the Military Joint Chiefs of Staff on all military intelligence issues.

Department of the Navy Office of Naval Intelligence

The Office of Naval Intelligence is the oldest United States intelligence agency. It was established in 1882. The Office of Naval Intelligence specializes in the collection of intelligence, intelligence production and dissemination of vital, timely and accurate maritime-related technical, geopolitical and military and naval intelligence. The Office of Naval Intelligence headquarters is located in Suitland, Maryland.

America is a maritime nation whose prosperity and national secu-rity depend on the free navigation of the world's oceans. To provide this prosperity and national security the Office of Naval Intelligence is there to ensure naval dominance globally, prevent hostile acts against the United States, protect maritime-related population centers and critical maritime infrastructures and to safeguard the ocean and its resources. This is accomplished through the Office of Naval Intelligence that oper-ates the Nimitz Operational Intelligence Center, the Farragut Technical Analysis Center, the Kennedy Irregular warfare Center and the Hopper Information Services Center (Figure 2.4).

United States Marine Corps Intelligence Division

As a part of the United States Department of the Navy the United States Marine Corps Intelligence Division has the responsibility to establish pol-icy, plans, budgets and staff supervision of all Marine Corps intelligence activities. The United States Marine Corps Intelligence Division is also responsible for Geospatial Intelligence, SIGINT, Human Intelligence, and Counterintelligence. The Division ensures that there is an effective single synchronized strategy for the development of Marine Corps Intelligence, Surveillance and Reconnaissance for global tactical operations. The United States Marine Corps Intelligence Division works closely with the Office of Naval Intelligence.

Figure 2.4 Dr. Daniel J. Benny during his time as Naval Intelligence Officer with the Office of Naval Intelligence (Official U.S. Navy Photograph).

United States Coast Guard Intelligence

The mission of the United States Coast Guard Intelligence as one of the United States military services and as part of the Department of Homeland Security is to: *"Conduct intelligence activities to provide timely, objective, relevant, and actionable maritime intelligence to drive operations, enable mission support, and inform decision making for Coast Guard and Homeland Security missions and National Security requirements."*

The United States Coast Guard Intelligence operates the Maritime Intelligence Fusions Centers that provide intelligence for all United States Coast Guard Districts and Sectors. The Maritime Intelligence Fusions Centers incorporate the use and participation of members of state and local law enforcement as well as member of other military organization and federal law enforcement and intelligence services. This intelligence sharing with other organizations increases cooperation and the collection and analysis of vitae maritime intelligence to protect the United States homeland.

The United States Coast Guard Intelligence operates the nation's Coast Guard Response Center and the America's Waterways Watch Program. The America's Waterway Watch is a public outreach program encouraging participants to simply report suspicious activities to the Coast Guard and/or other law enforcement agencies. The goal is to seek the participation of all members of the maritime industry such as tow-boat operators, recreational boaters, marina operators or others who live, work or engage in recreational activities around America's waterways by participating in its America's Waterway Watch program, a nationwide initiative similar to the well-known and successful Neighborhood Watch program that asks community members to report suspicious activities to local law enforcement agencies (Figure 2.5).

Individuals who spend time on or near the water already know what is normal and what is not and are well suited to notice suspicious activities possibly indicating threats to the United States homeland security. Participants in the America's Waterway Watch should adopt a heightened sense of awareness toward unusual events or individuals you may encounter in or around ports, docks, marinas, riversides, beaches or waterfront.

Department of the Army Intelligence and Security Command

The Department of the Army Intelligence and Security Command provides intelligence for the United States Army. It also supports the Military

Figure 2.5 A large United States Coast Guard Intelligence America's Waterways Watch banner hanging at the Long-level Marina in Wrightsville, Pennsylvania (Photograph by: Dr. Daniel J. Benny).

Joint and Coalition commands. In addition, the United States Army Intelligence and Security Command provides intelligence to other agencies of the United States Intelligence Community as needed.

The United States Army Intelligence and Security Command executes its intelligence mission command of operational intelligence and the Army's security forces. The United States Army Intelligence and Security Command conducts, synchronizes and also integrates its global multi-discipline and all-source intelligences as well in relationship to global security operations. The United States Army Intelligence and Security Command provides advanced intelligence-related skills and training to include linguistic, acquisition support, logistics and specialize communication capability. This is in support of the Military Joint and Coalition commands and other agencies of the United States Intelligence Community.

Department of the Air Force Intelligence

Within in the United States Air Force there are several organizations that provide intelligence. These organizations include the Office of the Deputy of Staff, Intelligence, Surveillance and Reconnaissance, the Twenty-Fifth Air Force and the Air and Space Intelligence Center. These United States Air Force organizations provide multisource intelligence, reconnaissance and surveillance intelligible for strategic and tactical use. These organizations also work closely with the National Security Agency related to cryptologic activities.

United States Space Force Intelligence

Created in December 2019 the United States Space Force was operational on October 1, 2020. Its intelligence component became the newels member of the United States Intelligence Community. According to the Space Force:

> *Space has become essential to our security and prosperity. Space systems are woven into the fabric of our way of life and is fundamental to our economic system. From the satellites that power the GPS technology that we use every day, or allow us to surf the web and call our friends, or enable first responders to communicate with each other in times of crisis, or orchestrate transactions in the world financial market, or even allow us to use credit cards at gas stations.*

The goal of the Space Force Intelligence is to train and organize as well as equip space forces for the protection of the United States and its allies in space operations. It also provides space capabilities to our joint military forces.

Review Exercise

Describe the intelligence role of each of the United States military intelligence services should there be a sea, air and ground war with China.

REFERENCES

9/11 Commission. 2004. *The 9/11 Commission Report*. New York: W.W. Norton & Company.

Best Jr., Richard. 2014. "Leadership of the U.S. Intelligence Community: From DCI to DNI," *International Journal of Intelligence and Counterintelligence* Volume 27, Issue 2. http://ezproxy.ap s.edu/login?url=http://dx.doi.org/10.1080/08850607.2014.872533

Burger, Charles. 2019. "Maritime Security: The Uncharted Politics of the Global Sea," *International Affairs* Volume 95: 971–978.

Clark, Robert. 2011. *The Technical Collection of Intelligence*. Washington, DC: CQ Press.

Clark, Robert. 2013. *Intelligence Analysis: A Target-Centric Approach*. Washington, DC: Sage.

Hammond, Thomas H. 2010. "Intelligence Organizations and the Organization of Intelligence," *International Journal of Intelligence and Counterintelligence* Volume 23, Issue 4.

Keegan, James. 2008. "Intelligence in War," *RUSI Journal* Volume 152 (2008): 27.

King, Dave. 1981. "Intelligence Failures and the Falkland's War," *Intelligence and National Security Journal* Volume 2, Issue 2: 14–17.

Lowenthal, Mark and Clark, Robert. 2016. *The 5 Disciplines of Intelligence Collection*. New York: SAGE.

Office of the Director of National Intelligence. (ODNI). 2013. *U.S. National Intelligence: An Overview*. Washington, DC: ODNI.

Richelson, Jeffery. 2016. *The US Intelligence Community*. Boulder, CO: Westview Press.

Stavridis, James. 2017. *Sea Power: The History and Geopolitics of the World's Oceans*. New York: Penguin Books.

Warner, Michael. 2014. *The Rise and Fall if Intelligence*. Washington, DC: Georgetown University Press.

3

United States Key Allied Intelligence Services

UNITED KINGDOM INTELLIGENCE COMMUNITY

The United Kingdom Intelligence Community comprises several agencies that include civilian intelligence services, law enforcement and military. The civilian services include the Secret Intelligence Service (MI6), Security Service (MI5) and Government Communications Headquarters (GCHQ). There is also the Metropolitan Police Scotland Yard, which is a law enforcement agency. The final component is the military's Defense Intelligence (DI).

Secret Intelligence Service (MI6)

The United Kingdom's Secret Intelligence Service was established in July 1906. The secret Intelligence Service works secretly around the world to ensure the safety of the United Kingdom by using cutting edge technology and espionage to counter the adversaries. The three core aims of the Secret Intelligence Service are stopping terrorism, the disruption of the activity of hostile states and giving the United Kingdom a cyber advantage. The MI6 headquarters is located in Vauxhall, London, England (Figure 3.1).

The Secret Intelligence Service works closely with Britain's Security Service (MI5), GCHQ, Metropolitan Police Scotland Yard and the DI. The Secret Intelligence Service also works closely with the United States Intelligence Community and the intelligence services of other allied nations.

DOI: 10.4324/9781003270843-3

Figure 3.1 Secret Intelligence Service (MI6) Headquarters, London, England (Photograph by Dr. Daniel J. Benny).

Security Service (MI5)

The United Kingdom's Security Service was established in October 1990. The Security Service provides security and intelligence within the United Kingdom with its headquarters located in London, England. The role of the Security service is to protect the United Kingdom's national security. This includes protection against terrorism, espionage, sabotage and the activity of agents of foreign powers and adversary nations. The Security Service also provides protection from those with the intent to overthrow or undermine the nation's parliamentary democracy form of government by industrial, political or violent means (Figure 3.2).

The Security Service works closely with the Secret Intelligence Service (MI6), GCHQ, Metropolitan Police Scotland Yard and the DI. The Security Service also works closely with the United States Intelligence Community and law enforcement agencies as well as the intelligence services and law enforcement agencies of other allied nations.

Figure 3.2 Security Service (MI5) Headquarters, London, England (Photograph by Dr. Daniel J. Benny).

Government Communications Headquarters

The GCHQ was established on November 1, 1919 under the name of Government Code and Cypher School during World War I. During World War II the organization worked out of Bletchley Park and broke the German Enigma codes. It was later named the Government Communications Headquarters. The headquarters is located in Cheltenham, England with four other locutions in the United Kingdom.

The current missions of the GCHQ through Singles Intelligence are to Counter Terrorism by stopping terrorist attacks in the United Kingdom and the nation's interest overseers. The prevention of Cyber Security attacks against the United Kingdom ensures that the United Kingdom has the strategic advantage in dealing with threats from hostile nations. The organization also supports the national defense by providing protection for defense personnel and all of the United Kingdom's military assets in support of war fighting. The goal of the GCHQ is to use *"Our brilliant people use cutting-edge technology, technical ingenuity and wide-ranging partnerships to identify, analyse and disrupt threats to the UK."*

Metropolitan Police "Scotland Yard" Directorate of Intelligence

The Metropolitan Police was established by Sir Robert Peel in 1829. The original headquarters was located in four Whitehall Place. That location had been the site of a residence owned by the Kings of Scotland, known as "Scotland Yard." Based on that address the Metropolitan Police have come to be known as Scotland Yard. The Metropolitan Police provide law

Figure 3.3 Ten Downing Street, London England – the residence of the Prime Minister of the United Kingdom, under the protection of Scotland Yard Special Branch (Photographs by Dr. Daniel J. Benny).

enforcement services in London, England. Scotland Yard also provides security and protective services to the Royal Family through its Special Branch to include the protection of 10 Downing Street in London the residents of the Prime Minster of the United Kingdom (Figure 3.3). All offers receive basic and advanced training at the Sir Robert Peel Police Academy outside of London, England.

The Metropolitan Police also provides law enforcement and security intelligence though it's Directorate of Intelligence. The intelligence provided is related to terrorism, organized crime, security, protective service and financial crime. The Directorate of Intelligence also provides intelligence analysis and scientific intelligence such as DNA collection and analysis.

Defense Intelligence

The DI is part of the United Kingdom's Strategic Command and provides intelligence products and assessments to the Minister of Defense. The intelligence provided is in support of the Royal Navy, Army Intelligence Corps, Army Royal Engineers and the Royal Air Force Intelligence.

The DI works closely with the United Kingdom's other intelligence services. This includes the GCHQ, MI5 and MI6. The organization also provides support to allied military services.

CANADIAN INTELLIGENCE COMMUNITY

The Canadian Intelligence Community is the closed physically located Allie to the United States located on the Northern border. The Canadian Intelligence Community comprises two organizations responsible for intelligence. They are the Canadian Security Intelligence Service (CSIS) and the Royal Canadian Mounted Police.

Canadian Security Intelligence Service

The CSIS was established in 1984 as the primary national intelligence agency for the Canadian government. It is responsible for intelligence collection, analysis, production and the dissemination of intelligence report and threats to the nation the Prime Minister of Public Safety. The CSIS is also the intelligence advisory agency to the Prime Minister of Public Safety.

The CSIS is authorized to conduct both covert and overt intelligence operations within the borders of Canada and abroad. The service has the intelligence responsibility to protect the nation from espionage, cyber-attacks, terrorism and internal domestic subversion against the government.

Royal Canadian Mounted Police

The Royal Canadian Mounted Police was established in 1873 as the North West Mounted Police. The name was changed to the Royal Canadian Mounted Police in 1920. The Royal Canadian Mounted Police is the primary national law enforcement agency in the Canada. The agency provides nationwide law enforcement investigative support-related criminal offenses as well as protective service to the government. The Royal Canadian Mounted Police also provide for the national security of Canada the investigation of espionage, terrorism and internal subversive threats to Canada. The Royal Canadian Mounted Police works closely with the CSIS as well as other nations' national law enforcement apparatus.

ISRAELI INTELLIGENCE COMMUNITY

The Israeli Intelligence Community comprises the Afaf Modin or Aman (IDF Intelligence) which is their military intelligence. Shabal (Shin Bet) covers internal intelligence and security. The Mossad is responsible for overseas intelligence. The three agencies of the Israeli Intelligence Community work together in order to protect the nation of Israel from foreign and domestic threats.

Agaf Modin or Aman IDF Intelligence

The IDF Intelligence was established on June 30, 1948. The IDF Intelligence is responsible for all intelligence related to the Israeli military and military operations. This includes strategic and tactical military intelligence collection, analysis and production. The intelligence is used by the Prime Minister and military command for political and military decisions.

Shabak or Shin Bet

Shin Bet was established on June 30, 1948. The role of Shin Bet is the internal intelligence and security of the nation of Israel. This included protection from terrorism, espionage and all subversive activities within the borders of the nation. Shin Bet is also responsible for the protection of Israeli government official.

Mossas

Mossas was established on March 2, 1951. Mossas mission is intelligence collection and counterintelligence outside the nation of Israel in order to protect the nation. This includes both overt and covert intelligence collection methods. The Mossas also takes part in special covert tactical intelligence operations worldwide that is in the interest of the nation of Israel.

GERMAN INTELLIGENCE COMMUNITY
BUNDESNACHRICHTENDIENST (BDN)

The BDN is the foreign intelligence service of the Federal Republic of Germany. It was founded during the Cold War period in 1956. The mission of the agency is to compile political, economic and military foreign intelligence for the protection of the Federal Republic of Germany.

Specific activity includes collection of open source and information beyond what is publicly available to include facts and opinions on critical issues. This accomplished with electron and human intelligence collection methods to include covert operations.

Bundesant fur Verfassungsschuts (BFV)

The BFV or the Federal Office for the Protection of the Constitution provided internal security and intelligence for the Federal Republic of Germany. This included threat from terrorism, espionage and subversion.

FRENCH INTELLIGENCE COMMUNITY

Directorate General for External Security (DGSE)

The DGSE was established on April 2, 1981 and its headquarters is located in Paris, France. The DGSE is France's foreign intelligence service operation out of country globally. The DGSE is responsible for the protection of France by means of intelligence collection, analysis and production. The service also conducted counterintelligence and paramilitary operations. Espionage against adversaries is another mission of the organization.

Directorate General for Internal Security (DGSI)

The DGSI was established on May 12, 2014 with its headquarters located in Levallois-Perret, France. The DGSI mission includes counterespionage, counterterrorism and counter cybercrime within the nation of France. It is also responsible for the monitoring and intelligence collection of subversive groups and organizations within France.

Directorate of Military Intelligence (DRM)

The DRM was established on June 16, 1992 and is under the Ministry of Defense. The DRM is the nation's military intelligence organization that is responsible for all strategic and tactical intelligence in support of the French Armed Forces. The DRM reports to the Military Chief of Staff and to the President of France who is also the Supreme Commander of the French military.

AUSTRALIAN INTELLIGENCE COMMUNITY

Office of National Intelligence (ONI)

The ONI advises the Prime Minister and National Security Committee on all intelligence matters vital to the national security. It overseas the National Intelligence Community. The ONI is accountable to the Prime Minster and the Cabinet.

Department of Home Affairs

The Department of Home Affairs is the interior ministry responsible for national security, law enforcement, border control, immigration, emergency management and internal intelligence matters.

Australian Secret Intelligence Service (ASIS)

The ASIS was established on May 13, 195 and its headquarters is located in Canberra, Australia. The ASIS is responsible for Australia's overseas intelligence service.

Australian Signals Directorate (ASDO)

The ASDO was established on November 12, 1947 and its headquarters is located in Canberra, Australia. The ASDO is responsible for all signals intelligence related to the intelligence community and the military. It also protects the nation from cyber security attacks against its communications and all other infrastructures.

Australian Geospatial Intelligence Organization (AGO)

The AGO was established on November 8, 2000 and its headquarters is located in Canberra, Australia. As part of the Department of Defense it is responsible for the collection, analysis and delivery of geospatial intelligence in support of the military and intelligence community for the protection of the nation.

Department of Foreign Affairs and Trade (DFAT)

The DFAT was established on July 24, 1987 and its headquarters is located in Barton, Australia. As subsidiary of the Intelligence Community it is responsible for foreign trade and counselor services with other nations to include intelligence issues.

Australian Security Intelligence Organization (ASIO)

The ASIO was established on March 6, 1949 and its headquarters is located in Canberra, Australia. The ASIO is the national internal intelligence and security service. Its mission is to protect the nation from espionage, terrorism, sabotage and subversive actions that threaten the nation.

Australian Federal Police (AFP)

The AFP was established on January 1, 1979. The AFP is the primary federal law enforcement agency for the investigation of cranial activities under the Department of Home Affairs.

Australian Transaction Reports and Analysis Center (AUSTRAC)

The AUSTRAC was established in 1989. It is responsible for the monitoring of financial transactions that could be linked to espionage, terrorism or other subversive crime and other activities against the nation.

JAPANESE INTELLIGENCE COMMUNITY

Public Security Intelligence Agency

The Japanese Public Security Intelligence Agency was established on July 21, 1952 and its headquarters is located in Chiyoda, Japan. The Japanese Public Security Intelligence Agency is the national intelligence agency for Japan under the Ministry of Justice. Its mission is to protect the nation from espionage, terrorism and subversive activities against Japan. This is accomplished by intelligence collection and analysis as well as intelligence investigations.

Review Exercise

Identify the United Kingdom intelligence services that would be involved in counterintelligence and counterterrorism operation within the United Kingdom and describe their activities to counter such threats.

REFERENCES

Allen, Thomas. 2008. *Declassified: 50 Documents That Changed History*. Washington, DC: National Geographic.

Andrew, Christopher. 2009. *Defend the Realm: The Authorized History of MI5*. New York: Alfred A. Kopf.

Colonna Vilasi, A. 2018. "The Israeli Intelligence Community," *Sociology Mind* Volume 8: 114–122. https://doi.org/10.4236/sm.2018.8200

Eisenburg, Dennis and Elilandau, Uri Dan. 1978. *The Mossad; Israel's Secret Intelligence Service Inside Stories*. New York: Signet.

Fido, Martin and Skinner, Keith. 1999. *The Official Encyclopedia f Scotland Yard*. London, England: Virgin Publishing.

Hearn, Chester. 2000. *Spies & Espionage A Directory*. San Diego, CA: Thunder Press.

Jeffery, Keith. 2010. *The Secret History of MI6*. New York: Penguin Press.

Richelson, Jeffery. 2016. *The US Intelligence Community*. Boulder, CO: Westview Press.

West, Nigel. 1995. *Historical Dictionary of British Intelligence*. Lanham, MD: Scarecrow Press.

4

Key Hostile Nations Intelligence Services

PEOPLE'S REPUBLIC OF CHINA INTELLIGENCE COMMUNITY

Ministry of State Security

The Peoples' Republic of China Ministry of State was established on July 1, 1983 and the headquarters is located in Beijing, China. The Ministry of States is China's primary intelligence, security and secret police agency. The Ministry of State is responsible for forgiven intelligence, counterintelligence and political security of the nation.

Intelligence Bureau of the Joint Staff

The People Liberation Army Intelligence Bureau of the Joint staff founded on August 1, 1927 is the intelligence apparatus of the Peoples' Liberation Army. The Intelligence Bureau of the Joint Staff is responsible for strategic and operational intelligence and includes China's military. This included ground forces, naval forces, air forces and rocket forces.

RUSSIAN FEDERATION INTELLIGENCE COMMUNITY

Foreign Intelligence Service of the Russian Federation

The Foreign Intelligence Service of the Russian Federation is the external intelligence service for the nation. It was founded in 1991 after the fall of

DOI: 10.4324/9781003270843-4

the Soviet Union and replaced the KGB. The headquarters is located in Moscow, Russia. The missions include espionage around the world in support of the Russian Federation.

Federal Security Service

The Federal Security Service is the primary internal security agency of the nation. It was founded in 1995 and the headquarters is located in Moscow, Russia. The missions of the Federal Security Service include counterintelligence, counterterrorism, border security and internal security. The organization is authorized to investigate violation of federal law.

DEMOCRATIC PEOPLE'S REPUBLIC OF KOREA INTELLIGENCE COMMUNITY

Reconnaissance General Bureau

The Reconnaissance General Bureau was founded in 2009. The organization is responsible for intelligence reconnaissance globally. The focus of its intelligence operation is on South Korea, Japan and the United States military and civilian targets.

Ministry of State Security

The Ministry of State Security was established in 1983. The Ministry of State Security is the nation's civilian intelligence, security and secret police organization of the nation. Its missions include counterintelligence, foreign intelligence and political security. The headquarters is located in Beijing, China.

Intelligence Bureau of the Joint Staff

The Intelligence Bureau of the Joint Staff is the military counterpart to the Ministry of State Security. It was established in 2016 and the headquarters is located in Dongsheng District, China. Its mission is the collection of military intelligence globally with a focus on the United States.

ISLAMIC REPUBLIC OF IRAN
INTELLIGENCE COMMUNITY
Islamic Revolutionary Guard Corps

The Islamic Revolutionary Guard Corps was founded on April 22, 1979 after the Iranian Revolution. The mission of the Islamic Revolutionary Guard Corps is to protect the national political system by means of counterintelligence activity. This includes foreign intervention as well as internal deviant movements within the nation.

Review Exercise

Research a current events situation involving an intelligence threat from Russia or China and provide an intelligence analysis of the specific intelligent threats to the United States for the nation selected.

REFERENCES

CIA. 2021. *CIA Factbook, China.* Langley: CIA.

CIA. 2021. *CIA Factbook, Iran.* Langley: CIA.

CIA. 2021. *CIA Factbook, North Korea.* Langley: CIA

CIA. 2021. *CIA Factbook, Russia.* Langley: CIA.

Cypher Brief. 2021. China Focuses Espionage on US College and Universities. Retrieved from China Focuses Espionage on U.S. Colleges and Universities (thecipherbrief.com).

DoD. 2020. *Military and Security Development Involving the Peoples Republic of China.* Washington, DC: Department of Defense.

FBI. 2021. *The Threat from China.* Retrieved from The China Threat — FBI.

Office of the Director of National Intelligence. (ODNI). 2013. *U.S. National Intelligence: An Overview.* Washington, DC: ODNI.

5

Categories of Intelligence

OPEN SOURCE (OPINT)

Open-source intelligence is the overt collection of information that is available publicly. This includes information from the media, internet, professional publications, academic publication, government documents, legal sources, commercial and corporate. Hard-to-find public information known as grey data is also available. Intelligence can also be obtained at public meeting locations and by dumpster diving. The is no legal risk to open-source intelligence collection as long as the information obtained is not protected, classified and stolen as that would be espionage. Espionage is illegal and convicted can result in fines and/or prison.

MEDIA

The media sources would comprise newspapers, printed news publications and magazine, television and radio news reports. Not all news information is accurate and it is often bias. With that said, it is a starting point in obtaining open-source information on current events. The information as always will need to be verified as to its accuracy.

INTERNET

An invaluable open source of intelligence can be obtained from the internet. Virtually any topic and organization can be researched on the

DOI: 10.4324/9781003270843-5

internet. One can search for information from government sites, private companies, professional organizations, social organizations, religious groups and institutions. A search can be made of individuals and even locations, maps and satellite photographs. This can be accomplished by using search engines, online databases, blogs, discussion groups and social media communications.

Various tools are available for open-source collection of intelligence on the internet. The most common search engines include Google, Dorks and Internet Explorer. Open-source software can also be obtained to streamline and even automate the search for information. This would include tools such as The Harvester or Shodan.

PROFESSIONAL PUBLICATIONS

Most of all professional organizations and societies have professional peer-reviewed journal or other types of publications. If one is seeking open-source intelligence on a specific group or specific information by locating a professional society or organization based on that topic, one can most often obtain those professional publications as a source of intelligence.

ACADEMIC PUBLICATIONS

Universities are hubs of research covering an array of topics. Unless the information is government research classified information or proprietary protected research information there is a wealth of open-source information from the academic community. This information is in the form of research studies, theses, dissertations, technical reports and peer-reviewed academic journal articles. There is also the opportunity to obtain information from academic forums, workshops and seminars. Spending time in public meeting places on campus can also be a source of intelligence.

GOVERNMENT

All government organizations, local, county, state and federal have open-source information that is available to the public. The information can be obtained from the government web sites, book or published reports.

LEGAL

Open-source intelligence can also be obtained from federal, state and local court filings on civil and criminal legal matters that are open to the public. This could include arrest records, domestic issues such as marriage and divorce records. Property records and corporate filings may also be obtained from federal, state and local court facilities.

COMMERCIAL AND CORPORATE

Commercial open-sourced information includes commercial and corporate data information based. Industrial and business assessments can also be of value. Commercial and corporate financial profiles are also available that can privies insight into a specific organization.

GREY DATA

Grey data is known as hard-to-find data that has been often discarded or no longer used but can still be accessed. Examples include business documents, technical reports, patents and a variety of unpublished information.

PUBLIC MEETING LOCATIONS

Open-source information can be obtained from public meeting locations. As an example if one wants to obtain information on an organization, they could visit a restaurant where many of the employees of the target organization meet each day before work or for lunch. Sitting next to this group information about the organization can be overheard. By doing this on regular bases the individual may think agent is an employee and even more information can be obtained in direct discussion with the company employees.

DUMPSTER DIVING

Dumpster diving is the process of sorting through the trash of an organization or individual to obtain intelligence. It is amazing what organization or individual will toss out in the rubbish that has critical information that can be utilized. Various states may of laws with regard to dumpster diving. It is important to know what the oval law is. As a general guideline if the trash is not on private property, at the curbside, it can be sorted though.

HUMAN (HUNIMT)

Human intelligence or HUNMIT is the oldest from of espionage and is considered the gold standard of intelligence collection. Human intelligence is the collection of information by intelligence officers from various intelligence assets who have access to critical intelligence. Human intelligence is so critical to the United States and its national security that the Central Intelligence Agency has within it organization a directorate related to the collection of human intelligence. There are several types of Human intelligence assets that can be exploited. These include targeted assets, walk-in assets and informants.

When dealing with human intelligence collection there is always a risk to the United States intelligence officers from enemy intelligence services of being identified that could result in capture or even death. There is a substantial risk to assets who spy for United States intelligence services.

TARGETED ASSETS

Targeted assets are individuals who are selected by an intelligence service as a source of intelligence. This type of asset is selected based on the type and value of intelligence they have access to and the ability to obtain and pass on that intelligence to the intelligence service. The individuals' position with the facility where the intelligence is sought is also a determining factor in who is targeted.

A targeted asset is one who in most situations does not want to provide the intelligible to an adversary intelligence service. These assets must be lured or forced to spy for an intelligence service. The asset can be lured by money, sex or other addictions they may have. The assets can be forced to spy through the use of blackmail. The targeted asset is placed in a compromising situation that is documented by video, photographs and sound recording. The asset is forced to spy or the compromising information is released to damage their situation.

WALK-IN ASSETS

A walk-in asset is one who approaches an intelligence service and offers to spy for them against their own nation. The motives vary but the number one motive is money. The money the walk-in asset seeks can be for a better lifestyle, to get out of debit or money to support addictions such as drugs, sex or gambling. The motive may be to get back at their nation or employer because they feel they were wronged in some manner.

A walk-in asset may offer to spy for personal reasons not relayed to money. The reasons could be ideological, political, social or religious. In this case they are offering their service to spy to correct r a wrong and/or fight back against the system in which they live. Walk-in assets can be very valuable. One needs to be alert that a walk-in asset is not a double agent seeking in compromise or infiltrate the other side's intelligence service.

INFORMANTS

Informants are individuals that an intelligence service can use to obtain information that they may have access to but not at the level of quality or importance that could be provided by an intelligence asset. An informant is paid in cash or rewarded in some other manner for the information they provide. Informants may be law-abiding individuals who work or have the ability to observe what is occurring at an area of interest by the intelligence service. Informants often have connections to criminal or terrorist organizations who will provide information for money or other benefits.

HUMAN INTELLIGENCE TRADECRAFT IN HOSTILE NATIONS

Human intelligence tradecraft is critical in obtaining vital intelligence from individuals in a position with access to the desired information. The most difficult aspect is the collection of intelligence in hostile nations. This has always been a challenge for the United States intelligence community. Hostile nations are those countries that pose a serious military, political, religious, economic or terrorism threat to the United States. There are currently five major hostile nations that pose various threats to the United States. Those nations include the People's Republic of China, the Russian Federation, the People's Democratic Republic of Korea, the Islamic

Republic of Iran and now the Islamic Emirate of Afghanistan. While the specific threats from each of those five nations vary, the threat from each singular nation is significant in their own right. The Peoples' Republic of China, the Russian Federation and the Democratic People's Republic of Korea are traditional hostile nations. The threat from those three nations is military, political and economic. The Islamic Republic of Iran and the Islamic Emirate of Afghanistan are hostile terrorist nations. The threat from those two nations is terrorism based in part on religious beliefs.

All of these states are considered totalitarian or autocracy in nature and are nations with limited access. Those facts hinder intelligence collection within those countries. Intelligence collection methods to include open-source intelligence, signals intelligence, geospatial intelligence as well as measurements and signature intelligence can be utilized against those nations without having the ability to penetrate borders of those hostile states borders. This is accomplished by the use of various United States intelligence community surveillance platforms operating outside of the hostile nations. Open-source intelligence can be obtained without being inside of a hostile nation through the review of publication, observations of news, media, social media and information placed on the internet.

The key intelligence collection problem is the ability to utilize human intelligence within those nations. The use of human intelligence to collect information is not an easy task in such environments. This is due to the fact that in order to obtain humane intelligence it is best to be able to have the physical placement of intelligence officers in those nations for purpose of intelligence collection. Intelligence officers in place within a hostile nation can be used to individually collect information. Most often the intelligence officers are used to facilitate the recruitment and handling of individual targeted living in those nations to become an asset for the United States intelligence community.

In order to effectively place intelligence officers within a hostile nation there must be a means of legitimate access to that country. Regarding the People's Republic of China and the Russian Federation there is a method of legitimate access to those two nations. The Unites States has embassies in each of those nations with Americans stationed at those locations. The United States embassies are used as a base of operation for intelligence collection. The United States State Department has staff members who are in a position to collect open-source intelligence within that nation.

At the United States embassies, the Central Intelligence Agency has intelligence officers on location. The Central Intelligence Agency intelligence officers are utilized for covert intelligence collection. The covert intelligence collection used by the Central Intelligence Agency includes human intelligence collection methods. This could include intelligence collection directly by the intelligence officer. Most often the goal is to recruit foreign nationals as an asset from that target nation who would be able to provide a long-term source of high-quality intelligence.

As previously stated, the collection of human intelligence is not easily accomplished but is a problem that needs to be solved. Human intelligence on the ground in those nations is critical to the national security of the United States. Allen Dulles, the first civilian director of the Central Intelligence Agency, stated human intelligence on the ground in the target nation is the best source of information as long as the source has been vetted and is reliable. It was also his belief that the best human source is one who is not engaging in spying for money or due to being blackmailed but rather based on that individual's belief that is it just the right things to do for whatever reason.

Attempting to obtain human intelligence within the Democratic People's Republic of Korea as a traditional hostile nation as well as the Islamic Republic of Iran and the Islamic Emirate of Afghanistan that are hostile terrorist nations is more of a challenge. There is no diplomatic presence in those nations in the form of a United States embassy. Due to the lack of an in-county physical base of operation there are no United States State Department staff to collect open-source intelligence. There is also no in-county physical base of operation that can be used by the Central Intelligence Agency.

Because of this situation it is not feasible to place Center Intelligence Agency intelligence officers in those nations to collect intelligence first hand or to recruit foreign nationals as assets of those nations to collect intelligence while on the ground in those nations. In order to solve this problem so that human intelligence can be obtained on the ground in the Democratic People's Republic of Korea the Islamic Republic of Iran and the Islamic Emirate of Afghanistan other more creative means must be deployed in order to obtain the human intelligence from those nations. Solving the issue is critical to the national security of the United States.

In those three extremely challenging nations the Central Intelligence Agency must resort to the recruitment of foreign nationals from the Democratic People's Republic of Korea, the Islamic Republic of Iran and the Islamic Emirate of Afghanistan by making contact with such individuals when they travel outside of their home nation. Recruitment can also be accomplished by other covert means of communication with the foreign national in those nations. Third-party individuals who are not United States intelligence officers and do have access to those nations could be recruited to identify and then contact foreign nationals in those nations for possible recruitment. Once recruited the third-party individual could also be utilized to facilitate the passing on of information or to retrieve information from those assets in those nations. Various human intelligence collection methods are utilized for the recruitment of foreign nationals to spy on their nation. The tradecraft that will be used depends on the situation.

IMAGERY (IMINT)

Imagery intelligence is the capturing of objects of interest that are reproduced by optical means on film, reproduced electronically, electronic display devices. Radar and infrared sensors as well as lasers are utilized for imagery collection. There are numerous methods of collecting imagery. Traditional handheld cameras' film and now digital can be utilized to collect imagery intelligence. Cell phones are an excellent tool for covert imagery collection and they do not look out of place. Small spy cameras have been used in the past. The original MINOX film spy camera used in the 1960s was small and very effective. For covert collection a later digital version of the famous MINOX spy camera was developed (see Figures 5.1 and 5.2).

Imagery intelligence can be national, civil or commercial. National is imagery produced by the United States intelligence community or military. Civil is imagery produced by governmental agencies both federal and state for non-intelligence and non-military use but could be of value to the intelligence community. Commercial is imagery produced by the private sector and can also be of value to the intelligence services.

Imagery sensors include visible, infrared, radar and multi-spectral. Visible sensors are best utilized in daylight conditions and are excellent for detailed analysis due to the high resolution of the images. It is restricted to daylight use and cannot penetrate vegetation on the ground. Infrared sensors are excellent for night and clear weather imagery collection with good picture resolution and require a skilled analysis for interpretation of the imagery. Radar sensors are very effective in all weather conditions day or night. It also requires a skilled analysis for interpretation of the imagery. Multi-spectral sensors are most effective for intelligence mapping and analysis of the terrain and require a skilled analysis for interpretation of the imagery.

Figure 5.1 One of the original MINOX spy cameras from Dr. Daniel J. Benny's collection (Photograph by Dr. Benny).

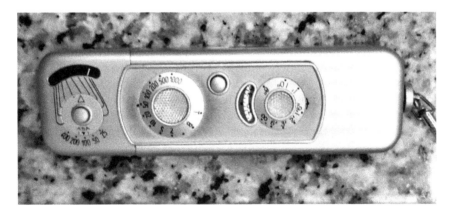

Figure 5.2 A new version of the original MINOX spy cameras from Dr. Daniel J. Benny's collection (Photograph by Dr. Benny).

The collection methods or platforms for intelligence collection can be handheld by individual with a camera. Stationary collection is when imagery surveillance equipment is placed at a location and is operated automatically or remotely. Aerial collection involves the use of civilian, military or spy aircraft such as the SR-71 with camera systems mounted on the aircraft

Figure 5.3 SR-71 at the United States Air Force Armament Museum in Fort Walton Beach, Florida (Photograph by Dr. Daniel J. Benny).

(see Figure 5.3). Unmanned Aerial Systems are an excellent source of both low and higher altitude imagery collections. Intelligence satellites are a critical platform for intelligence imagery collection on the global scale.

GEOSPATIAL (GEOINT)

Geospatial intelligence was created in 2005 by the United States intelligence community. Geospatial intelligence is the visual representation of intelligence activity on the globe. The final intelligence product is derived from an integration of imagery intelligence, geospatial information and nonliteral intelligence analysis of spectral spatial and other temporal fused elements.

Geospatial intelligence data can be obtained by focusing on stationary or moving intelligence targets by the use of electro-optical, synthetic radar and other intelligence sensors used by the United States intelligence community. The goal is to be able to explore and analyze imagery and geospatial intelligence in order to visually depict various physical features as well as providing geographically referenced intelligence activities at any location on the globe.

SIGNALS (SIGINT)

Signals intelligence is the collection of foreign intelligence derived from information and communications systems. This included collection from foreign communications such a telephone, cell telephones and email. Other intelligence collection sources include radar and various electronic systems.

Signals intelligence also includes the analysis of foreign communication in various languages and dialects. Often these communications are transmitted in codes or the use of other communication security measures. Signals intelligence applications are utilized to break these codes and penetrate other security measures that have been put in place to protect the communications systems.

MEASURES AND SIGNATURES (MASINT)

Measures and Signatures intelligence is technical intelligence derived from qualitative and quantitative data analysis. It uses specific sensors to identify distinctive aspects related to the source, sender or emitter of the intelligence target. Measures and Signatures intelligence includes radar, acoustic, nuclear and radio frequency/electromagnetic pulse intelligence. Measures and Signatures intelligence also included laser, electro-optical, spectroscopic, directed energy weapons and unintentional radiation intelligence.

Measures and Signatures intelligence can be used to identify enemy weapons platforms and systems. This would include submarines and surface watercraft. Both ground- and air-launched missile systems can also be identified using Measures and Signatures intelligence. Nuclear weapons testing can be identified using Measures and Signatures intelligence.

INTELLIGENCE TRADECRAFT AND OPERATIONS CASE STUDIES

The Bay of Pigs of 1961 and the Cuban Missile Crises of 1962

Bay of Pigs Covert Operation
The Invasion
During the President Dwight D. Eisenhower administration the United States was involved in the Cold War with the Soviet Union and the spread of communism around the globe. With the communist takeover of Cuba by Fidel Castro it was of grave concern to the United States intelligence community and President Dwight D. Eisenhower to have communist

nation backed by the Soviet Union, only 90 miles from Key West, Florida. This was considered a national security threat to the United States.

In 1959 Allen Dulles the Director of the Central Intelligence at that time in history devised a covert Central Intelligence Agency plan to remove the Fidel Castrol regime from power and rid the island nation of communism. The premise of the covert operation was to have exiled Cubans who left and escaped from Cuba after the Castro administration gained power who were at that time residing in the United States carrying out the liberation plan. The Central Intelligence Agency recruited and trained the Cuban exile a counter-revolutionary force known as the Brigade. The forces consisted of over 1,500 Cuban exiles.

According to the plan devised by the Central Intelligence Agency the Cuban exile force would conduct an invasion from sea at the location known as the Bay of Pigs on the island of Cuba. The force would be supported by air power using B-26 bomber aircraft operated by Cuban exiles marked to appear to Cuban aircraft that were operated by Cuban defectors. There was also to be United State Naval support should it be required.

It was believed that the invasion by the Cuban exiles would be known to the people of Cuba as it was taking place and that it would create an uprising of the Cuban people and take down the Castro Communist government and restore the nation to the people. President Dwight D. Eisenhower approved the plan as the cover operations preparations began in the last months of the Eisenhower administration.

With the election of the new President John F. Kennedy his administration inherited the cover operation that was developed by the Central Intelligence Agency. Upon review of the plan President John F. Kennedy authorized the Central Intelligence Agency to continue with the planned invasion. The invasions began on April 15, 1961 with an aerial bombardment of the Castro Air Force using eight B-26 bombers panted to look like Cuban aircraft and flown by Central Intelligence Agency trained Cuban exile pilots. On the initial bomb run they failed to destroy all of the Cuban Air Force aircraft. There was to be a second air strike by the sane eight B-26 bombers. A ninth B-26 aircraft flew into Miami airport in Florida with bullet holes in the fuselage of the aircraft in a ruse to make it appear to the world believe that the pilots and aircraft was a defector from Cuba and that it was involved in the air attack against Cuba. This was to reinforce the concept that the other eight aircraft were also defector aircraft from Cuba and to hide the United States' direct involvement in the invasion.

The landing area from the sea was to occur before dawn. The area at the beach where the landing was to take place had a large amount of coral beneath the water. The coral hindered the small watercraft and, in some situations, damaged the watercraft. Some of the watercraft sank. This delay caused the landing force to arrive at the beach daylight and not in darkness as planned. At the time of the beach landing the B-26 bombers conducted an air strike against the Cuban air force aircraft parked on the ground. The air attack by the B-26 bombers failed to destroy all of the Cuban air force aircraft. The Cuba air force was able to respond and attack the invasion on the beach. The Cuban air force strikes killed many of the Cuban exile invasion force and the rest of the force were trapped on the beach. They could not move inland or retreat by sea. The Castro Air Force attacked the invasion forces supply ship that was off shore form the Bay of Pigs landing site.

President John Kennedy was asked by the Central Intelligible Agency to approve a second air strike by the B-26 bombers to support the exiles trapped on the beach. President John Kennedy refused to authorize the second strike at that time. The Central Intelligence and the United States Navy requested additional support from the United States Navy or the United States Air Force in the form of air strikes. President Kennedy then did agree to have several United States Navy aircraft provide cover for another attack by the B-26 bombers now being flown by United States military pilots. The jets were to provide cover for the B-26 bombers but due to a mix-up in the time, the B-26's arrived early without jet air cover and two were shot down with four American pilots killed. Castro recovered the bodies as proof that the United State was behind the invasion. Without the addition of military support any chance of the invasion succeeding was doomed. By April 16, 1962 with the advance of the Cuban ground forces on the Cuban exiles located on the beach were killed and survivors were taken as prisoners. By April 16, 1961 the failed invasion had ended.

By this time the world was aware of the invasion and the role of the United States with regard to the Cuban exiles and the B-26 bombers. The Cuban government had the bodies of the American pilots and the aircraft that were shot down as evidence. Another piece of evidence of the United States involvement was the B-26 bomber flown to Miami airport. The media looked at the aircraft and noted that the gun barrels were mounted at the incorrect location and there was tape left on the barrels where they were pained. That destroyed the ruse that it was a defector aircraft from Cuba and the revelation was broadcast worldwide by the media.

In the end many in the member of the invasion force were killed and the rest ended up in prison in Cuba. Because the invasion force never made it off the beach, there was no uprising of the people as envisioned by the Central Intelligible Agency. The cover operations developed by the Central Intelligence Agency known as the Bay of Pigs Invasion was not only an intelligence and military failure but also political failure for President Kennedy and the United States.

Intelligence Failures
The overt operation could have been successful. Had there been effective intelligence analysis and competent mission planning Cuba could have been free of communist rule. The following intelligence failures have been identified based upon a review of the various after-action investigations of the failed Bay of Pigs Invasion.

Plausible Deniability
The Central Intelligence Agency a covert operations that started out as a guerrilla support mission for the invasion over time developed into a overt an overt armed conflict consisting of a beach landing and air strikes. The Central Intelligence Agency failed to establish effective plausible deniability for the United States regardless if the invasion worked and more importantly if it failed. The world knew immediately that the United States was involved in the Bay of Pigs Invasion plan.

There was also the lack of details about the Cuban air force B-26 bombers and the weapons placement on the aircraft. This inaccuracy was noted immediately by the media when the B-26 was flown into Miami airport by the Cuba exiles as ruse of the aircraft being a Cuban military pilot and aircraft defection. This destroyed that attempt of plausible deniability. The use of American pilots on the second air attack mission was also a failure of plausible deniability when two aircraft were shot down and Cuban had the bodies of the American pilots.

Cuban Forces Capabilities
There was a failure to collect effective intelligence with regard to the capabilities of the Cuban air and ground forces. This included size of the Cuban air force and ground forces and how fast they could respond to an invasion. The lack intelligence and details about the Cuban air force B-26 bombers and the weapons placement on the aircraft as previously mentioned demonstrated the lack of effective intelligence collection on the Cuban air force.

Lack of Proper Communication and Command and Control
The Central Intelligence had insufficient Spanish-speaking instructors to train the Cuban exiles in the United States who would comprise the

invasion force. This created a communications weakness. There was poor analysis related to the need for proper training facilities and material resources. The lack of training contributed to failed communications and lack of effective command and control of the operatives and the mission. An example of this was the mistiming of the air support for the second B-26 air strike where two aircraft were lost. Due to the lack of jet air support for the B-26 bombers, overall, there was insufficient employment of highly qualified staff, poor communication with exile leaders and other staff of the invasion force and United States government agencies.

Bay of Pigs Landing Site
There was a failure of intelligence to effectively analyze the physical landing site at the Bay of Pigs where the invasion force would come ashore. The United States intelligence community photographs of the invasion location showed dark areas in the water. Due to improper analysis, the dark areas were thought to be seaweed which would cause no issues with the small landing watercraft. The dark areas were in fact coral under the water. As the small watercraft enter the Bay of Pigs the coral damaged and sunk several of the watercraft delayed the planned predawn beach landing. Because of this failure of the intelligence analysis and not being able to identify the coral under the water the invasion force landed on the beach in daylight and was comprised.

Internal Resistance in Cuba
There was the failure on the part of the Central Intelligence Agency to satisfactorily organize internal resistance in Cuba. One of the goals of the mission was for there to be an uprising of the people when the Cuban exile force landed on the island. That uprising was then expected to provide support for the exiles' landing force. Because the Central Intelligence Agency failed to organize such a resistance movement in Cuba prior to the invasion there was no such uprising by the people. The assumption that the Cuban people would respond in that manner and take to the streets was itself another intelligence analysis fiasco.

Operational Security
In any intelligence and military mission operational security is critical so that the enemy does not obtain intelligence on the mission plan. Operational security was another intelligence failure. There was the lack of foresight and operational security controls and due to the fact that there were so many Cuban exile involved over several months of preparation

and training in the United States that it should have be assumed that intelligence would be leaked and Fidel Castor. Reports indicated that some intelligence of the planed invasion was leaked to Fidel Castro and he became aware of the invasion. It was also reported that he did not have all of the details such as the date and location of the invasion.

Lack of Contingency Planning

The final intelligible failure was the lack of credible contingency plans to effectively deal with the various setbacks that did occur during the covert operation and the actual invasion of Cuba. There was no effective contingency plan to deal with the problem of the coral in the water and the impact on the watercraft. There was contingency plan related to the B-26 bomber ruse at Miami airport that was compromised by the media. There were contingency plans to deal with the failed first B-26 bomber attack to run a second B-26 bomber attack. The most serious failure in the contingency plans was that there was no method to rescue the trapped exile force on the beach at the Bay of Pigs.

Conclusion

The plan to have Cuban exiles trained and supported by the Central Intelligible Agency invaded Cuba to take down the communist government of Fidel Castro and restore freedom to Cuba was a noble plan. That leads to the question. Did ineffective intelligence analysis by the Central Intelligence Agency lead to the failure of the Bay of Pigs Invasion? The hypotheses are that due to the ineffective intelligence analysis and assessments made by the Central Intelligence Agency, the covert Bay of Pigs Invasion failed.

When examining all the intelligence failures identified during the Bay of Pigs Invasion that include plausible deniability, Cuban forces capabilities, lack of proper communication and command and control, the Bay of Pigs land site, internal resistance in Cuba, operational security and the lack of contingency planning. It is clear that the Central Intelligence Agency did not utilize effective and proper intelligence analysis in planning and executing the Bay of Pigs Invasion by Central Intelligence Agency-backed Cuban exiles.

The fallout from this disaster was enormous. The Kennedy administration and the United States were seen as a failure. Fidel Castro was still in command of Cuba. The Cuban exiles were killed and others in prison. Allen Dulles was fired as Director of the Central Intelligence Agency, and the reputation of the Central Intelligence Agency was damaged.

The most serious aspect of the failed Bay of Pigs Invasion is that it set the stage for Cuban Missile Crisis in October 1962. With the communist regime of Field Castro who was supported by communist Soviet Union viewed the attempted invasion of Cuba by the United States as a serious threat. The rational of Cuba and the Soviet Union to counter such a threat was to have the Soviet Union place short-range nuclear missiles on the island of Cuba only 90 miles from the United States.

The placement of nuclear missiles in Cuba by the Soviet Union was detected by the United States intelligence community in October 1962 using U-2 Spy aircraft. At that point there was a standoff between the United States and the Soviet Union. The United States demanding that the Soviet Union remove the nuclear missiles from Cuba. This incident that inched the United States and the Soviet Union too close to a nuclear is known as the Cuban Missile Crises of October 1962.

The failure of the Central Intelligence Agency to effectively analyze all of the intelligence related to the Bay of Pigs Invasion in April of 1961 not only led to the failure of that mission but also to the a nuclear showdown with the Soviet Union a little over a year later in October 1962. Had the Bay of Pigs mission succeeded, Fidel Castor would have been removed from Cuba and it would not have been a communist satellite of the Soviet Union. The Soviet Union would not have positioned nuclear missiles in Cuba and there would not have been a Cuban Missile Crises. This sequence of event demonstrates that failed intelligence analysis can not only have a negative impact on a current operation but also a negative impact into the future.

THE CUBAN MISSILE CRISES

The Cuban Missile Crises occurred in October 1962. After the failed Bay of Pigs, the Soviet Union made a secret deal with Cuba to install Soviet nuclear missiles in Cuba. By the fall of 1962 United States U-2 aircraft photographed the evidence of Soviet nuclear missiles in Cuba during a routine surveillance flight. On September 4, 1962 President Kennedy issued a public warning about offensive missiles in Cuba. On October 14, 1962 additional surveillance flights showed the continued construction of Soviet missile sites in Cuba. The Joint Chiefs of Staff and some advisors supported an air strike to take out the missile and an invasion of Cuba. (In my view that is what should have taken place, the Soviets would have done nothing.) Kennedy ordered a quarantine of Cuba on October 22, 1962. He did not call it a blockade as that would be considered a state of war and calling it a quarantine allowed the United Sates to receive support from the Organization of American States. The United State was now at DEFCON 3.

On October 26, 1962 a United States surveillance aircraft was shot down over Cuba. The United States prepared for invasion of Cuba but continued with secret talks with the Soviet Union. On October 27, 1962 the Soviet Union said to would remove the missiles from Cuba if the United States would remove its Jupiter missiles from Turkey near the Soviet Union. Kennedy responded that if the Soviet Union would remove the missiles from Cuba the United States would not invade that nation. The United States said it would remove the missiles from Turkey as it was planning to do but that must not be part of any public agreement. On October 28, 1962 the crises was over.

The Cuban Missile Crises was in part a success. United States intelligence did detect the missiles and that was good intelligence analysis. In the end the crises ended without going to war. The Central Intelligence Agency did not foresee the placement of missiles that was a failure. It appears there was effective Central Intelligence Agency communication with the White House just as with Bay of Pigs incident. "Did the blockade make war more likely or less likely?" It was not a blockade but was a quarantine, there is a legal difference. It did increase the tension but it had to be done to show determination on the part of the United States. The removal of the United States missiles from Turkey was the quid pro quo and it was kept secret to save political face of Kennedy who after the Bay of Pigs was seen as soft on the Soviet Union.

With regard to a nuclear war over Cuba, my view is that was just a lot of "missile" rattling. We should have taken out the missiles with air strikes and invaded Cuba the Soviets would not have stared a nuclear war over it. That is the nice thing about the Mutual Assured Destruction Doctrine.

THE RATIONAL CHOICE THEORY AND INTELLIGENCE OPERATIONS – FALKLAND ISLANDS WAR OF 1982

The Rational Choice Theory

The Rational Choice Theory is a criminology theory that has been used in the criminal justice profession for many years. The concept of the theory is that an individual considering a criminal act be it traditional crime, organized crime or even terrorism will go through a process to assess the risk of their actions. The perpetrator must assess if the act can be achieved without them being identified, taken into custody for prosecution or sustaining injury or death.

If the target of the perpetrators' criminal act has effective security that could result in those individuals being identified, taken into custody for prosecution or sustaining injury or death, then they will not proceed against that target. The perpetrators will select a softer target with little or no security. In that case they have made a rational choice that it was not to their benefit to take part in a crime against that target.

A historic example of the use of the Rational Choice Theory related to intelligence, national security and military operations is the Falkland Islands War of 1982. The Rational Choice Theory can be applied to most any situation to include the decision by Argentina to invade the Falkland Islands in 1982. It can also be applied to the decision of the United Kingdom to respond to the invasion and to take back the Falkland Islands.

The issue that will be explored in the case study based on the Rational Choice Theory did Argentina use to assume that there will be a low risk of failure when they invaded the Falkland Islands. That same issue will be explored related to the United Kingdom in assuming that there would be a low risk of their failure to retake the Falkland Islands.

The analysis and findings of this case study examined the usefulness of intelligence during the war. It also explored the application of the Rational Choice Theory related to the activity of Argentina and the United Kingdom during the Falkland Islands War preceding the start of the conflict and during the Falkland Islands War. Throughout the research an exploration of the decisions made by the two nations and how the Rational Choice Theory may have been utilized related the intelligence issues.

The case study explores the outcome of the war based on the intelligence and use of the Rational Choice Theory will be analyzed. The success of British and Argentine intelligence during the Falkland Islands War will also be evaluated in relation to the application of the Rational Choice Theory.

Historical Overview of the Falkland Island War

For many years Argentina felt that the Falkland Islands that they called the Malvinas should be part of Argentina and not Britain in part since the islands lay 200 mile off the coast of Argentina. The Argentine government felt that the United Kingdom took control of the Falkland Islands over a century before as part the imperial acts of the then British Empire.

In 1982 the Argentine government was having serious economic unrest and the population was protesting the government and the military junta led by Galtieri. To redirect the peoples focus on the faulting government it was believed by the leaders in Argentina that if they were to take the Falkland Islands, the people of Argentina would then support the government and that would end the unrest.

This assessment by the government was correct and when they did take the Falkland Islands, the people rallied around the Argentine government. This support lasted until Argentina lost the Falkland Islands War and the people then once again turned on the Argentine government and against the Galtieri regime. The loss of the Falkland Islands War was the final push to remove Galtieri and military junta from office that in 1976 seized control of the nation from Isabel Peron.

On April 2, 1982 the Falkland Islands War began when Argentinean military forces invaded the Falkland Islands by sea. On April 3, 1982 the Argentinean forces were able to take control of and occupy South George Island with troops and control of the all of the islands as well as the small contingent of Royal Marines and the British subject who lived on the islands. Argentina also now had control of the sea around the Falkland Islands.

Britain responded decisively with the support of the British people. On April 4, 1982 the HMS Conqueror sailed from Faslane, Scotland. The HMS Invincible and HMS Hermes sailed from Portsmouth, England on April 5, 1982 along with the Royal Marines.

By April 11, 1982 two British submarines arrived at the Falkland Islands. They were the HMS Spartan and HMS Splendid. On April 12, 1982 Britain declared an Exclusion Zone of 200 nautical miles around the Falkland Islands to seal off the islands from additions enemy ships.

On April 14, 1982 Britain began the assault to retake the Falkland Islands by sea with the Royal Navy and by land with the Royal Marine and members of the SAS. After a month of fierce sea, air and ground assaults and the loss of British and Argentine ships, on June 14, 1982 the Argentine military surrendered to British forces and the Falkland Islands were once again under the control of the United Kingdom. With the victory by the British forces the Falkland Islands War ended.

Looking through the lens of history one could argue that it was obvious a high risk for the government of Argentina to invade the Falkland Islands. One needs to look through the lens of the Argentina government in the spring of 1982 to fully examine the Rational Choice Theory and the decision to invade the Falkland Islands.

Rational Choice Theory and Argentine Intelligence During the War
There are intelligence issues related to the Falkland Islands War where the
Rational Choice Theory can be applied related to the decision of Argentina
to invade the Falkland Islands. As previously mentioned the national sov-
ereignty of the Falkland Islands had been in dispute for year between the
United Kingdom and Argentina.

In 1982 at the time of the war the Falkland Islands were under the
control of the United Kingdom. The Argentine government made what
they thought were rational choices based on the intelligence available to
them at the time and invaded the Falkland Islands to secure the islands to
incorporate them as part of Argentina.

When exploring the Rational Choice Theory as it is related to and can
be applied to the decision by the government of Argentina to invade the
Falkland Islands, there are several issues that emerge. At that time in history the people of Argentina were protesting the government and the rul-
ing class. The leader of the Argentine government believed that if they
took action to regain the Falkland Islands, the people would then support
the Argentine government and the protest against the government protest
would cease. Using the Rational Choice Theory it was worth the risk to
take back the Falkland Islands if such action would end the government
protest and the people would support the government.

The government of Argentina also supposed that their nation was correct in that the Falkland Islands belonged to and were a part of Argentina
and that the Falkland Islands were stolen from Argentina by Britain during the period of history when the British Empire ruled. With that mindset
on the part of the Argentine government and the belief of the Argentine
government that the United Kingdom may accept the premise that the
Falkland Islands were indeed stolen by Britain years early and not con-
test the invasion and not respond with the military to secure the Falkland
Islands from Argentina. Since the Rational Choice Theory is based on
assessing risk the Argentina government made the decision that the risk
of the United Kingdom responding with the military to take back the
Falkland Islands was minimal.

The Argentine government made what can be considered another
rational choice decision. The decision was that even if the United
Kingdom did not accept the premise that the Falkland Islands did indeed
belong to Argentina that because the United Kingdom was 7,916 miles
from the Falkland Islands the United Kingdom would not attempt to
take the Falkland Islands back by force using the military. Once again
the Argentina government made the rational choice decision that the risk

of the United Kingdom being able to or willing to respond 7,916 miles to engage the Argentine military was not that high.

The final issue was that if the United Kingdom did attempt to take the Falkland Islands back because of the distance the British military would need to cross and related supply chain issues that the United Kingdom could be easily defeated by the Argentine military operating relatively close to the nation of Argentina. Based on those assumptions the Argentine government would have made the rational choice that the risk of failure was very low to invade the Falkland Islands as they did on April 2, 1982.

With the lack of effective and current intelligence the government of Argentina underestimated Prime Margaret Thatcher, the resolve of the British people, the Royal Navy, the Royal Marines and the SAS. On June 14, 1982 the SAS and the Royal Marines with the support of the Royal Navy recaptured the Falkland Islands from the Argentina military.

Even if a nation utilizes the Rational Choice Theory and believes the risk to be low it does not mean that the nation suitably evaluated the risk. With regard to the view that the people of Argentina would support the government if they invaded the Falkland Islands they were correct. The people rallied around the nation and government leaders. What the Argentine government failed to equate in the decision was what the reaction would be if they failed to take back the Falkland Islands. When Argentina lost the Falkland Islands War the people once again tuned on the government and the leaders were removed from office.

The Argentine government intelligence failed. The United Kingdom did not concede, they did send the Royal Navy, Royal Marines and the SAS 7,916 miles. In the end the United Kingdom defeated Argentina and regained control of the Falkland Islands.

One might say that not all decisions made using the Rational Choice Theory ended up being rational. This could be true especially if the intelligence use in that decision is nonexistence or flawed as was the case with regard to Argentina intelligence and the Falkland Islands War.

Rational Choice Theory and British Intelligence During the War

The United Kingdom was taken by surprise with the invasion of the Falkland Islands by the Argentina government's military forces. This was an oblivious lack of intelligence on the part of the British with regard to the unrest against the government of Argentina within that nation. British intelligence and the government did not foresee the possibility that the Argentine government would use an invasion to the Falkland Islands as an instrument to rally the people of Argentina around the government and diminish the government unrest within that nation.

Once the invasion of the Falkland Islands occurred the United Kingdom began diplomatic talks with Argentina to mitigate the situation. At the same time Prime Minister Margaret Thatcher and the British government had to make a rational choice decision with regard to sending British military forces to retake the Falkland Islands. The decision was made to send military forces to the Falkland Islands to take back the islands as talks continued. The military forces comprised the Royal Navy, Royal Marines and the SAS.

The rational choice to send the military forces to the islands included the view that a diplomatic solution would be reached before the British forces actually arrived at the Falkland Islands. Another element of the rational choice to send military forces to the Falkland Islands was that Britain believed that such a show of force in itself could end the conflict without actual military action. Based on historical accounts many of the British service members in route to the Falkland Islands believed that they would not actually be involved in an armed conflict and that a show of force would result in the retreat of Argentine military forces from the Falkland Islands and end the conflict.

Prime Minister Margaret Thatcher believed that if in fact the British forces had to engage in combat to take back the Falkland Islands from Argentina then they would triumph in that effort.

In the end the Argentine government and their military did not reach a diplomatic agreement and the Argentina military did not abandon the Falkland Islands just because Britain was sending a military force. Britain did however make a successful rational choice to send the military force to the Falkland Islands and defeated the Argentine military on the sea and on the land and took back the islands and won the Falkland Islands War of 1982.

The Rational Choice Theory can also be applied to the development of intelligence sources by the British during the Falkland Islands War. During the Falkland Islands War the British needed human sources (HUMNT) on the ground at St. George Island. St. George Island was the primary location of the Argentine ground troops after the invasion of the islands.

The Argentine troops had to be defeated not only on the sea but also on the ground at St. George Island in order to recapture the Falkland Islands. This task to defeat the Argentine military at St. George Island was assigned to the Royal Marines and SAS to fight the ground war against the Argentine military forces. The British military were able to obtain HUMINT sources on St. George Island from the British residence who lived on the island. Communication was established by means of HAM radios that some of the residence on St. George Island had. The British made the rational choice that there would be a low risk to utilize the residences as a HUMIT intelligence sources. That British also made the rational choice that with the aid of the British citizens on the island as HUMIT intelligence source their assault on the Argentine troops on St. George Island would bring victory.

That rational choice made by the British military worked. The HUMIT intelligence on the ground at St. George Island provided critical intelligence as to the location of Argentine troops and their movements. That intelligence was critical to the Royal Marines and the SAS on the ground and contributed to the defeat of the Argentine troops on the St. George Island (West, 1989). The end results were the United Kingdom winning the war against Argentina and retaking the Falkland Islands in that final and decisive land battle against Argentina troops on St. George Island.

CONCLUSION

The case study comprised an examination of the effectiveness of decisions of the United Kingdom and Argentina related to the possible application of the Rational Choice Theory in their decision related to the Falkland Islands War of 1982. Based on the results of the research it is plausible that the Argentina government used the Rational Choice Theory in their decision to invade the Falkland Islands to deflect the decent of their citizen against the government of Argentina.

The Argentina government also utilized the Rational Choice Theory in their belief that the risk would be low because in their view, the British government would not attempt to take back the Falkland Islands in their mindset due to Britain's lack of will to fight. The distance of the Falkland Islands from the United Kingdom and the logistics to travel and fight a war from that distance was also a factor. Argentine also felt that the risk was low because if the United Kingdom did send military to the Falkland Islands, the Argentine government and military believed that they could win the war against Britain.

During the research the use of the Rational Choice Theory by the United Kingdom is plausible based on the following factors. The government of the United Kingdom upon looking at the risk felt it would not be best for their national honor to not act and take back the Falkland Islands. The British government also believed that the risk was low in being able to travel to the islands and support the supply chain to facilitate the war operations.

The British government and military also felt that the risk was low to send military because that the show of force may lead to a diplomatic resolve of the situation. The United Kingdom had the view that if British action against Argentina to take back the Falkland Island that the war would end in victory for the United Kingdom.

With regard to the intelligence aspect of the war and the use of the Rational Choice Theory it could also have been applied to the development of intelligence sources by the British during the Falkland Islands War. During the Falkland Islands War the British military required human sources (HUMNT) on the ground at St. George Island. This is because St. George Island was the primary location of the Argentine military on the ground after the invasion of the Falkland Islands.

The British military understood that the Argentine military troops would need to be defeated not only on the sea but also on the ground at St. George Island. This was critical in order to recapture all of the Falkland Islands and win the war. The British military were in a position to obtain HUMIT sources on ground at St. George Island. The intelligence could be obtained from the British residence who lived on the island. Communication between the British military and the citizens on St. George Island was established by means of HAM radios. HAM radio was a primary means of communication by the citizens on the Falkland Islands. The British Royal Marines and SAS were able to use that vital intelligence to defeat the Argentine troops on the Falkland Islands and ending the 1982 Falkland Islands War.

Based on the research it is apparent that the Rational Choice Theory could have been applied by both the Argentina government and military and the British government and military in their decisions related to the Falkland Islands War.

REVIEW EXERCISE

Identify the various categories of intelligence that could be used to track the activities of an attack by the Russian Federation on Eastern Europe.

REFERENCES

Abell, Peter. 1991. "Rational Choice Theory," *Journal of Sociology* 53–957606: 21–24.

Akers, Ronald. 1990. "Rational Choice Deterrence Theory in Criminal Justice," *Journal of Criminal Law and Criminology* Volume 81, Issue 3: 73–39.

Ambrose, Stephen, 1981. *Ike's Spies*. New York: Doubleday.

Boyce, George. 2006. "The Falklands War," *English Historical Review* Volume CXXI, Issue 491: 32–36.

Burger, Charles. 2019. "Maritime Security: The Uncharted Politics of the Global Sea," *International Affairs* Volume 95: 971–978.

Clark, Robert. 2011. *The Technical Collection of Intelligence*. Washington, DC: CQ Press.

Dulles, Allen. 1963. *The Craft of Intelligence*. New York: Harper & Row.

Fischer, Robert. 2005. *Introduction to Security*. New York: Elsevier.

Goldman, Jan. 2006. *Ethics of Spying: A Reader for the Intelligence Professional*. Lanham: Scarecrow Press.

Hammond, Thomas H. 2010. "Intelligence Organizations and the Organization of Intelligence," *International Journal of Intelligence and Counterintelligence* Volume 23, Issue 4.

Hoover, J. Edgar. 1958. *Masters of Deceit*. New York: Holt, Rinehart & Winston.

Hoover, J. Edgar. 1962. *A Study of Communism*. New York: Holt, Rinehart & Winston.

Keegan, James. 2008. "Intelligence in War," *RUSI Journal* Volume 152 (2008): 27.

King, Dave. 1981. "Intelligence Failures and the Falkland's War," *Intelligence and National Security Journal* Volume 2, Issue 2: 14–17.

Lehman, John. 2012. "The Falkland's War," *RUSI Journal* Volume 157, Issue 6: 80–85.

Lowenthal, Mark. 2009. *Intelligence: From Secrets to Policy*. Washington, DC: CQ Press.

Middlebrook, Martin. 2012. *The Falklands War*, South Yorkshire: Pen & Sward Books.

Navy Post Graduate School. 2004. *Falklands War Cause and Lessons*. Monterey: Defense Technical Information Center.

Office of the Director of National Intelligence. (ODNI). 2013. *U.S. National Intelligence: An Overview*. Washington, DC: ODNI.

Richelson, Jeffery. 2016. *The US Intelligence Community*. Boulder, CO: Westview Press.

Roos, Dave. 2020. *5 Reason Why the Bay of Pigs Invasion Failed*. Accessed November 7, 2020, 5 Reasons Why the Bay of Pigs Invasion Failed | HowStuffWorks.

Shapiro, Ian. 1997. *Rational Choice Theory*. London: Sage. https://dxdoi.org/10.4135/9781473976177

Speller, Ian. 2012. *Understanding Naval Warfare*. New York: Routledge.

Stavridis, James. 2017. *Sea Power: The History and Geopolitics of the World's Oceans*. New York: Penguin Books.

Tietzen, Katelyn. 2014. "After Thirty Years: The Falkland Wat of 1982," *All Theses* 1020: http://tigerprints.clemson.edu/all_theses/192

US Department of State. 2021. *The Cuban Missile Criss October 1962.* Accessed November 7, 2021 Milestones: 1961–1968- Office of the Historian (state. gov).Warner, Michael. 2014. *The Rise and Fall if Intelligence.* Washington, DC: Georgetown University Press.

West, Nigel. 1989. *The Secret War for the Falkland Islands: SAS MI6 and the War Whitehall Nearly Lost.* New York: Warner Books.

Wyden, Peter. 1979. *The Bay of Pigs: The Untold Story.* New York: Simon & Shuster.

6

Intelligence Collection, Processing, Analysis and Dissemination Methods

CENTRAL INTELLIGENCE AGENCY INTELLIGENCE CYCLE

The Central Intelligence Agency Intelligence Cycle has been the traditional method utilized by the Central Intelligence Agency. It has also been utilized by other intelligence organizations of the United States intelligence community. The five steps in the Central Intelligence Agency Intelligence Cycle include Planning and Direction, Collection, Processing, All-Source Analysis and Production and Dissemination.

Planning and Direction

Before intelligence is collected a determination needs to be made as to what intelligence the customer is seeking. Based on the specific requirements of the customer planning needs to take place in order to identify the source of the intelligence to be collected. Direction on how the intelligence will be collected must be provided for the intelligence operation to be successful.

Collection

Collection is the physical gathering of the intelligence utilizing the various methods of collecting to include Open Source (OPINT), Human (HUNIMT),

DOI: 10.4324/9781003270843-6

Imagery (IMINT), Geospatial (GEOINT), Signals (SIGINT) and Measures and Signatures (MASINT) as discussed in Chapter 5 of this book.

Processing

The processing stage is the conversion of the massive volume of information collected to a usable from by the analysts. This would include data reduction, language translations and data reduction so that the information can be effectively analyzed.

All-Source Analysis and Production

At this stage of the intelligence cycle there has been a conversion of the initial information obtained into a finished intelligence product ready to be presented to the customer. This conversion occurs by analyzing the information to ensure that the information has relevance and accuracy and is non-bias, reliable and usable and timely. The intelligence is put into context and a coherent whole to be used by the customer. The final product would include assessment, judgments and implications to be used by the customer.

Dissemination

The final step in the Central Intelligence Agency Intelligence Cycle is the dissemination of the finished intelligence product to the customer. Based on the final intelligence product the customer may feel that additional intelligence is required. This would then trigger the start of the intelligence cycle once again.

Director of National Intelligence Intelligence Cycle

The Director of National Intelligence Intelligence Cycle includes six steps in its intelligence cycle. The six steps include Planning, Collection, Processing, Analysis, Dissemination and Evaluation.

Planning

In the planning stage the policy makers and customers make a determination as to what intelligence issues need to be addressed. Intelligence priorities are then established and the decision on what United States intelligence agencies will collect the required information.

Collection

Collection is the physical gathering of the intelligence utilizing the various methods of collecting to include Open Source (OPINT), Human (HUNIMT), Imagery (IMINT), Geospatial (GEOINT), Signals (SIGINT) and Measures and Signatures (MASINT).

Processing

The processing stage is the conversion of the enormous bulk of information collected to a usable format. This would include data reduction, language translations, and data reduction so that the information can be effective analyzed.

Analysis

The analysis involves and examination and evaluation of the collected information and to add context to the information as to integrate it into the final usable intelligence product. The final product would include assessment, judgments and implications to be used by the customer.

Dissemination

The final intelligence product is delivered to the customer. An example is the President's Daily Brief covers the current intelligence situations.

Evaluation

The evaluation stage involves a review of the final intelligence product for relevance, accuracy, bias and timeliness. At this stage there is feedback from the customer. If more intelligence is required by the customer the intelligence will begin once again to obtain and provide the new information.

Target-Centric

The target-centric approach to intelligence was introduced by Robert Clark in his book *Intelligence Analyst: A Target-Centric Approach*. What he provided to the intelligence community was an alternate methodology of Central Intelligence Agency and Director of National Intelligence traditional intelligence cycles. The target-centric method completely changes the intelligence progression to a collaborative process between the collectors of intelligence, the analysis of intelligence and the customer as one cohesive network. The target-centric approach was used by General Stanley A. McChrystal during the Iraq War. He defined the target-centric approach as "F3EA" that stands for:

Find: This is where the target be it an individual or a physical location is identified as a source of intelligence.

Fix: The target of the intelligence operations is placed under continuous surveillance until positive identifies are verified.

Finish: Assign agents to collect the intelligence in the field.

Exploit: Intelligence is obtained, secured and mined for useable data.

Analyze: The information is then analyzed for usefulness and dissemination.

At any point in this process the intelligence collectors, the intelligence analysis and the customer of intelligence can step in and seek additional information that starts the process over again.

REVIEW EXERCISE

Select two of the three intelligence methods discussed in this chapter, the Central Intelligence Agency, the Director of National Intelligence and the Target Centric and compare and contrast the difference between the two selected.

REFERENCES

Ambrose, Stephen. 1981. *Ike's Spies*. New York: Doubleday.

Best Jr., Richard. 2014. "Leadership of the U.S. Intelligence Community: From DCI to DNI," *International Journal of Intelligence and Counterintelligence* Volume 27, Issue 2. http://ezproxy.apus.edu/login?url=http://dx.doi.org/10.1080/08850607.2014.872533

Clark, Robert. 2011. *The Technical Collection of Intelligence*. Washington, DC: CQ Press.

Clark, Robert. 2013. *Intelligence Analysis: A Target-Centric Approach*. Washington, DC: Sage.

Criswell, John. 2020. *Research Design*. New York: SAGE.

Hammond, Thomas H. 2010. "Intelligence Organizations and the Organization of Intelligence," *International Journal of Intelligence and Counterintelligence* Volume 23, Issue 4. http://ezproxy.apus.edu/login?url=http://dx.doi.org/10.1080/08850601003780987

Keegan, James. 2008. "Intelligence in War," *RUSI Journal* Volume 152 (2008): 27.

Lowenthal, Mark. 2009. *Intelligence: From Secrets to Policy*. Washington, DC: CQ Press.

Lowenthal, Mark and Clark, Robert. 2016. *The 5 Disciplines of Intelligence Collection*. New York: SAGE.

Office of the Director of National Intelligence. (ODNI). 2013. *U.S. National Intelligence: An Overview*. Washington, DC: ODNI.

Richelson, Jeffery. 2016. *The US Intelligence Community*. Boulder, CO: Westview Press.

Warner, Michael. 2014. *The Rise and Fall if Intelligence*. Washington, DC: Georgetown.

7

Determining the Value of Intelligence

SOURCES

The sources of intelligence can come from any of the intelligence collection methods previously discussed that include Open Source Intelligence (OPINT), Human Intelligence (HUNIMT), Imagery Intelligence (IMINT), Geospatial Intelligence (GEOINT), Signals Intelligence (SIGINT), and Measures and Signatures Intelligence (MASINT).

RELIABILITY

The reliability of intelligence is determined by the sources and information provided. The vital consideration is the sources and information obtained be trusted to be what it is purported to be. Determining the reliability is based on the type of intelligence, how it was obtained, the past history of the reliability of information from the collection method and source. The cross-referencing of information obtained with additional collection methods and sources can confirm or dispute the intelligence that has been received.

DOI: 10.4324/9781003270843-7

RELEVANCE

The relevance of intelligence refers to the information related to the matter at hand. The information must be connected to what the customer is seeking or to the intelligence mission. If there is no correlation between the intelligence and what is needed then that information is of no intelligence value in that specific situation.

TIMELINESS

What is intelligence one day may be of no value the next day. For intelligence to be of value it must be obtained and available at the time when it is most needed. This is especially true in critical situations necessary to the national security of the nation.

ACCURACY

For intelligence to be useful and effective the intelligence provided needs to be as accurate as possible. The Intelligence Community needs to focus on gathering all the facts related to a specific mission. As Sherlock said *"There is nothing more important than trifler."*

OBJECTIVITY AND BIAS

Intelligence needs to be objective and free of bias. Intelligence analysis may have some sort of biases and various perceptions on all types of issues. When working in one's profession such as intelligence, it is critical to recognize those biases and various views on the subject matter at hand. By identifying those biases and different views one can then actively work to not allow the distortion of one's assessment related to the intelligence mission at hand. The structured analytic techniques such as the diagnostic technique can aid in dealing with biases and perceptions. Having worked in federal law enforcement, the Intelligence Community and having my private investigation business it is a mistake for investigators and intelligence analysis to develop a perceived view of what is taking place without first obtaining the facts. As Sherlock Holmes specified in *A Study in Scarlet* in 1987 over a 100 year ago *"It is a capital mistake to theorize before you have all the evidence. It biases the judgement."* In the readings this is identified as perceptual bias. The bottom line is that in these circumstances it prevents the intelligence analysis from obtaining the facts. By using various methods such as checking the assumptions, quality information checks, brainstorming or acting as a Devil's advocate it can allow the intelligence analysis to adjust their mindset to obtain factual information.

A historic example of biases and flawed perceptions was the decision by the United States intelligence and law enforcement community under President Franklin D. Roosevelt at the onset of World War II when he signed Executive Order 9066 on February 19, 1942. That executive order authorized the United States government to take into custody Japanese American citizens, having their homes and business confiscated and them being placed in concentration camps for the duration of the war. This was rationalized and justified because of their race and the perception that they would be a threat to the nation because the United States was at war with Japan. In the case of Minoru Yasui V. the United States this disgraceful event was up held by the United States Supreme Court who as author Mark Levin stated are *"just lawyers in black robes."*

As demonstrated in the historical example, see change basis in the Intelligence Community can be devastating. It can lead to false conclusions and missing the real threats that should be identified and acted upon by the Intelligence Community. Both of these outcomes do not serve the national security of the nation. It also does not serve the Professional integrity of the Intelligence Community.

USABILITY

In the end the intelligence provided by the Intelligence Community to the customer must be usable. If the intelligence is not useable then it is of no value. The final product needs to be what the customer was seeking and in a formation that can be useful based on the mission.

REVIEW EXERCISE

Provide examples of how intelligence can be tainted based on the information in this chapter.

REFERENCES

Doyle, Arthur Conan. 1887. *A Study in Scarlet. London*. England: Beeton's Christmas Annual.

U.S. Government. 2009. *A Tradecraft Primer: Structured Analytic Techniques for Improving Intelligence Analysis. Center for the Study of Intelligence*. Washington, DC: U.S. Central Intelligence Agency.

8

Intelligence Analysis

THE INTELLIGENCE ANALYSTS AND THE POLICYMAKERS

The role of the Intelligence Community analyst and the policymakers is critical in the national security decision-making process. The intelligence analysts work for the policymakers. To be successful at analyzing intelligence both the policymaker and the intelligence analysts must work together for the good of the mission and national security. Both parties must face the issues of what is reality and truth when it comes to intelligence. In other words what is the context of the intelligence. The intelligence analysts work in a different context than that of policymakers. The intelligible analysts' focus is the intelligence date and deriving reliable information and meaning form it. What the policymakers seek is reliable and actionable intelligible. Because taking action is a risk the policymakers expect superior reliability than that of the intelligence analysts. The greater the risk of failure, the policymakers expect more reliable intelligence.

The intelligence analysts must understand that the policymakers' decisions are based on other information not provided by the intelligence analysts. There are many different types of interest groups the policymakers must deal with. Because of that there is compromise and bargaining that take place. From the intelligence analysts' point of view bureaucratic politics should not be part of the scope of an intelligence analyst. That is where realty and truth must be confronted by the intelligence analysts.

To deal with this situation the "policy culture versus the intelligence culture" needs to be addressed. In each of the two cultures there are biases that will conflict. The intelligence analyst's role should be to help the

DOI: 10.4324/9781003270843-8

policymakers understand the situation by providing clear, accurate and timely intelligence. The intelligence analysts must also provide the policymakers with any ambiguities and uncertainties with reagreeing to the intelligence that has been provided even it is upsetting to the policymakers. There must also be an understanding of the intelligence analysts and policymakers' interaction. There needs to be effective rapport between the two but each must stay true to their role in the process. The policymakers must avoid negative influence on the intelligence analysts with pressure or tell them to follow the house line. In the end the intelligence analysts and the policymakers must work together with shared interests in providing the most accurate intelligence that will be usable for the policymakers.

TIMELINES

The timelines for intelligence collection can be critical to the Intelligence Community and the customer. What is intelligence today may be of no value tomorrow depending on the situation. The timeline needs to be established at the front end of the intelligence collection process in order to effectively plan for the collection of information and the analyzing of the information to meet the customers' schedule. The intelligence collection timelines may be short term or they may be long term.

Short Term

A short-term timeline is intelligence that it is needed within a critical timeline in order to effectively support the intelligence mission. The short-term timeline may vary from hours to days or even a few weeks based on the requirement of the situation. If there is a threat of an immediate attack of some sort then hours may be the effective timeline. To obtain intelligence on an issue for a customer before a vital meeting that is to be held within a few weeks then days or a week would be an acceptable timeline.

Long Term

A long-term timeline is intelligence that is not needed at the present time but may or will be of value in the future. Example would be the periodic imaging of an enemy nation's coastline to note any change in the features that would be relevant should there need to be a special operations landing on that coast. Another example is for the Intelligence Community to keep a current file on enemy nation naval officers, their movement and promotions, so in the event there would be the need for naval action against that enemy nation that there would be current intelligence about the naval officer who would be the adversary in such a conflict.

SCOPE

The scope refers to the area of consideration for the intelligence collection and operations. The scope will also depend on the specific mission related to the intelligence collection. It could be for political considerations, military force projection and in director support of ground-, naval-, air- or space-force operations.

Strategic

Strategic intelligence is looking at the global picture in relation to the national security of the United States. It is the evaluation of long-term trends and potential threats based on past experience and the current global situation. It is forward thinking. This may include intelligence that would be used by the customer for political and foreign policy issues involving other nation or regions of the world. It would also include the posturing of military and intelligence assets globally in or to be able to look over the horizon and to facilitate forward force projection around the globe.

Tactical

Tactical intelligence is the assessment of the immediate capabilities and weaknesses of adversary and enemy nations. It is also an examination of the intention of those adversary and enemy nations. This allows the United States to plan for any possible interactions with the threats and to allocate military or intelligence resources necessary to successfully confirm such threats in a timely manner.

Operational

Operational intelligence is real-time or close to real-time intelligence. This is the most critical type of intelligence as it has a very short life span for it to be useful. This would be in director support of active engagements in a conflict by ground-, air-, naval-, space- and cyber forces. It is the most high-pressure situation for intelligence collection and analysis as lives and the national security of the nation depend on it.

INTELLIGENCE DRIVERS

Intelligence drivers are what initiate the collection of intelligence by the Intelligence Community. There are four primary intelligence drivers. They are Customer Driven, Analysis Driven, Event Driven and Scheduled Drivers.

Customer Driven

Customer driven is when the Intelligence Community begins the collection of intelligence that is initiated by the customer. The customer presents the situation of concern and defines what intelligence is required to resolve the situation. Based on that request the Intelligence Community directs their assets to accomplish the intelligence mission.

Analysts Driven

Analysts driven is when the Intelligence Community intelligence analysts initiate the collection of specific intelligence. This is most often done during the routine collection of predetermined intelligence that the intelligence analysts are assigned to collect and identify additional information that may be of value.

Events Driven

Events driven is when there is a need to collect intelligence based on an event that is occurring or may be occurring in the near future. Examples include a threat of a terrorist attack, sudden activity of an enemy nation, military and special operation activities or counter espionage to eliminate an espionage threat.

Scheduled Driven

Scheduled driven are continuous areas of intelligence collection that is conducted on a predetermined timeline. This may include updating biographies of enemy nation naval officers, the number and type of enemy ships or weapons systems.

INTELLIGENCE MINDSET

The intelligence mindset refers to the mental attitude of the intelligence analysis. It is how the intelligence analysis sees the world and makes useful meaning of it. It is a mindset that allows the intelligence analysts to perform their intelligence duties in the most effective manner. The intelligence analysis should be inquisitive and persistent. The need to look over the horizon and be forward thinking and look at the issues from an external view.

With the proper mindset the intelligence analysis should know the end goal of the intelligence assignment and to ask what decision one needs to make to effectively develop and analyze the intelligence. Having the proper intelligence mindset allows the intelligence analysts to be able to view the work through various lenses and to be able to communicate with individuals who have diverse worldviews.

INTELLIGENCE PRODUCT

The intelligence product is the final presentation of the intelligence collected and analyzed that is provided to the customer. How the final product is presented will depend on what the customer requested. The final product will be a written intelligence report providing details of the intelligence collected and the result of the final assessment of that intelligence. The final report may be in hard copy form or electronic. The final product most often will include chart, graphs and photographs related to the intelligence collected. There may also be an oral presentation of the intelligence and assessments found in the final report. The oral presentation may be enhanced by the use of a power point presentation highlighting the information in the final report.

REVIEW EXERCISES

Provide real-world, current events examples of strategic, tactical and operations intelligence and describe how the intelligence in each situation would be of value.

REFERENCES

Bruce, James B. and George, Roger Z. 2014. *Analyzing Intelligence: National Security Practitioners Perspectives*. Washington, DC: Georgetown University Press.

Clark, Robert M. 2020. *Intelligence Analysis: A Target-Centric Approach*. Thousand Oaks, CA: CQ Press.

Cottam, Martha L., Beth Dietz-Uhler, Elena Mastors, and Preston, Thomas. 2010. *Introduction to Political Psychology*. 2nd ed. London: Psychology Press.

George, Roger Z. and Bruce, James B. eds. 2008. *Analyzing Intelligence: Origins, Obstacles, and Innovations*. Washington, DC: Georgetown University Press.

Klab, Cliff. 2022. *The Intelligence Mindset*. Washington, DC: The Academy of Completive Intelligence.

Lowenthal, Mark M. 2012. *Intelligence: From Secrets to Policy*. 5th ed. Los Angeles, CA: SAGE/CQ Press.

Renshon, Jonathan. 2009. "Assessing Capabilities in International Politics: Biased Overestimation and the Case of the Imaginary 'Missile Gap.'" *Journal Of Strategic Studies* Volume 32, Issue 1: 115–147.

"Thinking Like an Intelligence Analyst." n.d. Accessed December 3, 2015. http://webcache.googleusercontent.com/search?q=cache:Jo3y1_IKTncJ:werzit.com/intel/intel/papers/object134.doc+&cd=1&hl=en&ct=clnk&gl=us

9

Selected Intelligence Resources

PRIVATE PROFESSIONAL INTELLIGENCE ORGANIZATIONS

Private professional intelligence organizations and association are an excellent source of information related to intelligence operations. Through such organization's web pages, magazines, journals and newsletters, valuable information can be obtained.

The organizations also provide training, seminars, workshops and professional certifications. Memberships in such organizations are also an excellent source of networking and the exchange of valuable security and counterespionage information.

ASSOCIATION OF FORMER INTELLIGENCE OFFICERS

In 1975 the Association of Retired Intelligence Officer was formed. In 1978 the name of the organization was changed to Association of Former Intelligence Officers to reflect a pool of members who were not necessarily retired, which widened the pool of eligible members and reflects the current dynamic membership. The Association of Former Intelligence Officers has grown to over 5,000 members, with 24 active chapters across the United States.

A member of the Intelligence Community Associations Network the Association of Former Intelligence Officers is more than a professional or fraternal organization. Its distinguishing mission is educational, to reach

DOI: 10.4324/9781003270843-9

out to the public and explain what intelligence organizations do and to build a nationwide constituency for intelligence as a profession.

The mission of the Association of Former Intelligence Officers is to build a public constituency for a sound, healthy and capable U.S. intelligence system. Our focus on education fosters an understanding of the important role of intelligence in National Security and nurtures interest by students in careers in the many fields used by United States Intelligence Agencies. This includes the role of supporting intelligence activities in Unites States policy, diplomacy, strategy, security and defense. The Association of Former Intelligence Officers focuses on understanding the critical need for effective intelligence operations counterintelligence and security against foreign, political, technological or economic espionage, as well as covert, clandestine and overt counterterrorist or criminal operations threatening United States national security.

77 Leesburg Pike, Suite 324
Falls Church, Virginia 22043
Telephone: 703 790-0320
Email: afio@afio.com
Web page: https://www.afio.com

COLD WAR MUSEUM

The Cold War Museum was founded in 1996 by Francis Gary Powers Jr., son of famed U2 pilot Gray Francis Gary Powers. The museum is an excellent source of intelligence related to the Cold War period (Figure 9.1).

7412 Lineweaver Road
Warrenton, Virginia 20187
Telephone: 540 341-2008
Web Page: https://.coldwar.org

INTERNATIONAL ASSOCIATION FOR INTELLIGENCE EDUCATION

International Association for Intelligence Education was formed in June 2004 as a result of a gathering of 60 plus intelligence studies trainers and educators. This group, from various intelligence disciplines, including national security, law enforcement and competitive intelligence,

Figure 9.1 From the collection of Dr. Daniel J. Benny – photograph of the Cold War Museum Patch, Francis Gary Powers Jr and a check signed by famed U2 pilot Gray Francis Gary Powers (Photograph by Dr. Daniel J. Benny).

recognized the need for a professional association that would span their diverse disciplines and provide a catalyst and resources for their development and that of Intelligence Studies.

The purpose of International Association for Intelligence Education is to expand research, knowledge and professional development in intelligence education. This is accomplished by providing a forum for the exchange of ideas and information for those interested in and concerned with intelligence education, advancing the intelligence profession by setting standards, building resources and sharing knowledge in intelligence studies and fostering relationships and cultivating cooperation among intelligence professionals in academia, business and government.

P.O. Box 10508
Erie, PA 16514
Telephone: 814 323-6637
Email: Webmaster.iafie@gmail.com
Web page: https://www.iafie.org/

INTERNATIONAL SPY MUSEUM

The International Spy Museum is the only public museum in the United States solely dedicated to espionage and the only one in the world to provide a global perspective on an all-but-invisible profession that has shaped history and continues to have a significant impact on world events.

The Museum features the largest collection of international espionage artifacts ever placed on public display. Many of these objects are being seen by the public for the first time. These artifacts illuminate the work of famous spies and pivotal espionage actions as well as help bring to life the strategies and techniques of the men and women behind some of the most secretive espionage missions in world history.

The mission of the International Spy Museum is to educate the public about espionage in an engaging way and to provide a context that fosters understanding of its important role in and impact on current and historic events. The Museum focuses on human intelligence and reveals the role spies have played in world events throughout history. It is committed to the apolitical presentation of the history of espionage in order to provide visitors with non-biased, accurate information.

700 L' Enfant Plaza
Washington, DC 20024
Telephone: 202.393.7798
Email: info@spymuseum.org
Web page: https://www.spymuseum.org

NAVAL INTELLIGENCE PROFESSIONALS

The goal of the Naval Intelligence Professionals (NIP) is to further the knowledge of the art of maritime intelligence and to provide a vehicle whereby present and former NIP may be kept informed of developments in the Naval Intelligence community and of the activities and where-abouts of past shipmates. Founded in 1985 NIP is a nonprofit organization incorporated to enhance awareness of the mission and vital functions of the Naval Intelligence community as well as to foster camaraderie among NIP. It is an association of active duty, retired and reserve officers, enlisted personnel and civilians who serve or have served within the Naval Intelligence community, as well as those in certain other categories who qualify as a nonvoting subscriber.

NIP Executive Director
Post Office Box 11579
Burke, Virginia 22009
Email: naval.intelligence.pros@gmail.com
Web page: https://navintpro.org

PRIVATE PROFESSIONAL SECURITY ORGANIZATIONS

Private professional security organizations and association are an exceptional source of information related to security which is essential to the Intelligence Community and counterespionage program. Through such organization's web pages, magazines, journals and newsletters, valuable information can be obtained.

The organizations also provide security training, seminars, workshops and professional certifications. Memberships in such organizations are also an excellent source of networking and the exchange of valuable security information.

AMERICAN SOCIETY FOR INDUSTRIAL SECURITY INTERNATIONAL

The American Society for Industrial Security International is the preeminent society for security professionals. Founded in 1955 as the American Society for Industrial Security is dedicated to the security professionals by developing educational programs and publications that address security interests. This includes the American Society for Industrial Security International Annual Seminar and Exhibits. The American Society for Industrial Security International also publishes the industry's number one magazine *Security Management*. The American Society for Industrial Security Commission on Standards and Guidelines developed various security management standards and guidelines that are used by the security profession.

American Society for Industrial Security Certifications

American Society for Industrial Security International administers developed three internationally accredited certification programs. The Certified Protection Professional (CPP) board certification in security management

103

is recognized as the highest designation accorded a security practitioner. There is also the Apprentices Protection Professional. Two specialties certifications are also available: the Professional Certified Investigator and the Physical Security Professional (PSP).

1625 Prince Street
Alexandria, Virginia 22314
Telephone: 703-519-6200
Email: asis@asisonline.org
Web page: https://www.asisonline.org

ASSOCIATION OF BRITISH INVESTIGATORS

Formed in 1913, The Association of British Investigators (ABI) has been upholding professional standards in England for a century. The ABI campaigns tirelessly for regulation in the private investigative profession and promotes excellence, integrity and professionalism within its membership.

Brentano Suite, Catalyst House, Central Park
Elstree, Hertfordshire
WD6 3SY
England
Telephone: +44 (0) 2081917500
Email: secretariat@theaib.org.uk
Web page: https://www.theabi.org.uk

ASSOCIATION OF CERTIFIED FRAUD EXAMINERS

The Association of Certified Fraud Examiners is the world's largest anti-fraud organization and premier provider of anti-fraud training and education. With nearly 65,000 members, the Association of Certified Fraud Examiners is reducing business fraud worldwide and inspiring public confidence in the integrity and objectivity within the profession.

The Certified Fraud Examiner (CFE) credential denotes proven expertise in fraud prevention, detection and deterrence. CFEs around the world help protect the global economy by uncovering fraud and implementing processes to prevent fraud from occurring in the first place.

The Gregor Building
716 West Ave
Austin, TX 78701-2727 USA

Telephone: (800) 245-3321
Email: memberservices@acfe.com
Web page: https://acfe.com

COUNCIL OF INTERNATIONAL INVESTIGATORS

The Council of International Investigators was formed in 1955. The purpose of this meeting was to consider the formation of a close knit organization that they could trust to handle investigatory matters in their respective local areas. Emphasis was put on "Quality" not "Quantity." Qualified members can attain the designation of Certified International Investigate (CII).
POI Box 1015
St Helena, South Carolina 29920
Telephone: 1-917-292-0613
Email: lec@cii2.org
Web page: https://www.cii2.org

NATIONAL COUNCIL OF INVESTIGATION
AND SECURITY SERVICES

The objective of the council is to monitor national legislative and regulatory activities affecting the investigation and security industry. A substantial part of the Council's activities shall be to assist, advise, inform and influence legislation. Develop and encourage the practice of high standards of personal and professional conduct among those persons serving in the investigation and security industry.

Promote the purpose and effectiveness of investigation and security companies by any and all means consistent with the public interest. Subject to prior approval of the Board the Council may take a position and express an opinion on issues directly and generally affecting the investigation and security industry as such, provided, however, that no action shall be taken on such matters as clearly fall solely within the purview of an individual investigation or security company or a distinct group of investigation or security companies. To promote the private investigation and security industry and to educate members and the public in the advancement, improvement and uses of investigation and security services.

To assist local, state or regional groups of investigation and security companies in the common endeavor to advance and promote the investigation and security industry. To provide the opportunity for the exchange of experiences and opinions through discussion, study, the internet and publications. To cooperate in courses of study for the benefit of persons desiring to fit themselves for positions in the investigation and security industry, and to hold meetings and conferences for the mutual improvement and education of our members. To acquire, preserve and disseminate data and valuable information relative to the functions and accomplishments of investigation and security companies.

PO Box 200615
Evans, Colorado 08620
Telephone: (800) 445-8408
Email: inquire@nciss.org
Web page: https://www.ncis.org

WORLD ASSOCIATIONS OF DETECTIVES

The World Association of Detectives was founded in 1925. In 1950, the World Secret Service Association, Inc. was formed as a joint venture by the combined membership of the International Secret Service Association (founded in 1921) and the World Association of Detectives. At our annual conference in August 1966 in San Antonio, Texas, USA, our present name was unanimously approved by amendment, reverting to the name of "World Association of Detectives."

PO Box 200030
Evans Colorado 80620
Telephone: 443-982-4586
Email: bob@wad.net
Web page: https://www.wad.net

APPENDIX A
Espionage Act of 1917

SECTION 1

That:

    (a) *whoever, for the purpose of obtaining information respecting the national defence with intent or reason to believe that the information to be obtained is to be used to the injury of the United States, or to the advantage of any foreign nation, goes upon, enters, flies over, or otherwise obtains information, concerning any vessel, aircraft, work of defence, navy yard, naval station, submarine base, coaling station, fort, battery, torpedo station, dockyard, canal, railroad, arsenal, camp, factory, mine, telegraph, telephone, wireless, or signal station, building, office, or other place connected with the national defence, owned or constructed, or in progress of construction by the United States or under the control or the United States, or of any of its officers or agents, or within the exclusive jurisdiction of the United States, or any place in which any vessel, aircraft, arms, munitions, or other materials or instruments for use in time of war are being made, prepared, repaired, or stored, under any contract or agreement with the United States, or with any person on behalf of the United States, or otherwise on behalf of the United States, or any prohibited place within the meaning of section six of this title; or*

    (b) *whoever for the purpose aforesaid, and with like intent or reason to believe, copies, takes, makes, or obtains, or attempts, or induces or aids another to copy, take, make, or obtain, any sketch, photograph, photographic negative, blue print, plan, map, model, instrument, appliance, document, writing or note of anything connected with the national defence; or*

    (c) *whoever, for the purpose aforesaid, receives or obtains or agrees or attempts or induces or aids another to receive or obtain from any other person, or from any source whatever, any document, writing, code book, signal book, sketch, photograph, photographic negative, blue print, plan, map, model, instrument, appliance, or note, of anything connected with the national defence, knowing or having reason to believe, at the time he receives or obtains, or agrees or attempts or induces or aids another to receive or obtain it, that it has been or will be obtained, taken, made or disposed of by any person contrary to the provisions of this title; or*

    (d) *whoever, lawfully or unlawfully having possession of, access to, control over, or being entrusted with any document, writing, code book, signal book, sketch, photograph, photographic negative, blue print, plan, map, model, instrument, appliance, or note relating to the national defence, wilfully communicates or transmits or attempts to communicate or transmit the same and fails to deliver it on demand to the officer or employee of the United States entitled to receive it; or*

(e) *whoever, being entrusted with or having lawful possession or control of any document, writing, code book, signal book, sketch, photograph, photographic negative, blue print, plan, map, model, note, or information, relating to the national defence, through gross negligence permits the same to be removed from its proper place of custody or delivered to anyone in violation of his trust, or to be list, stolen, abstracted, or destroyed, shall be punished by a fine of not more than $10,000, or by imprisonment for not more than two years, or both.*

SECTION 2

Whoever, with intent or reason to believe that it is to be used to the injury or the United States or to the advantage of a foreign nation, communicated, delivers, or transmits, or attempts to, or aids, or induces another to, communicate, deliver or transmit, to any foreign government, or to any faction or party or military or naval force within a foreign country, whether recognized or unrecognized by the United States, or to any representative, officer, agent, employee, subject, or citizen thereof, either directly or indirectly and document, writing, code book, signal book, sketch, photograph, photographic negative, blue print, plan, map, model, note, instrument, appliance, or information relating to the national defence, shall be punished by imprisonment for not more than twenty years: Provided, That whoever shall violate the provisions of subsection:

(a) *of this section in time of war shall be punished by death or by imprisonment for not more than thirty years; and*

(b) *whoever, in time of war, with intent that the same shall be communicated to the enemy, shall collect, record, publish or communicate, or attempt to elicit any information with respect to the movement, numbers, description, condition, or disposition of any of the armed forces, ships, aircraft, or war materials of the United States, or with respect to the plans or conduct, or supposed plans or conduct of any naval of military operations, or with respect to any works or measures undertaken for or connected with, or intended for the fortification of any place, or any other information relating to the public defence, which might be useful to the enemy, shall be punished by death or by imprisonment for not more than thirty years.*

SECTION 3

Whoever, when the United States is at war, shall wilfully make or convey false reports or false statements with intent to interfere with the operation or success of the military or naval forces of the United States or to promote the success of its enemies and whoever when the United States is at war, shall wilfully cause or attempt to cause insubordination, disloyalty, mutiny, refusal of duty, in the military or naval forces of the United States, or shall wilfully obstruct the recruiting or enlistment service of the United States, to the injury of the service or of the United States, shall be punished by a fine of not more than $10,000 or imprisonment for not more than twenty years, or both.

SECTION 4

If two or more persons conspire to violate the provisions of section two or three of this title, and one or more of such persons does any act to effect the object of the conspiracy, each of the parties to such conspiracy shall be punished as in said sections provided in the case of the doing of the act the accomplishment of which is the object of such conspiracy. Except as above provided conspiracies to commit offences under this title shall be punished as provided by section thirty-seven of the Act to codify, revise, and amend the penal laws of the United States approved March fourth, nineteen hundred and nine.

SECTION 5

Whoever harbours or conceals any person who he knows, or has reasonable grounds to believe or suspect, has committed, or is about to commit, an offence under this title shall be punished by a fine of not more than $10,000 or by imprisonment for not more than two years, or both.

SECTION 6

The President in time of war or in case of national emergency may by proclamation designate any place other than those set forth in subsection:

(a) of section one hereof in which anything for the use of the Army or Navy is being prepared or constructed or stored as a prohibited place for the purpose of

109

this title: *Provided, That he shall determine that information with respect thereto would be prejudicial to the national defence.*

SECTION 7

Nothing contained in this title shall be deemed to limit the jurisdiction of the general courts-martial, military commissions, or naval courts-martial under sections thirteen hundred and forty-two, thirteen hundred and forty-three, and sixteen hundred and twenty-four of the Revised Statutes as amended.

SECTION 8

The provisions of this title shall extend to all Territories, possessions, and places subject to the jurisdiction of the United States whether or not contiguous thereto, and offences under this title, when committed upon the high seas or elsewhere within the admiralty and maritime jurisdiction of the United States and outside the territorial limits thereof shall be punishable hereunder.

SECTION 9

The Act entitles "An Act to prevent the disclosure of national defence secrets," approved March third, nineteen hundred and eleven, is hereby repealed.

APPENDIX B
United States Economic Espionage Act of 1996

SECTION 1. SHORT TITLE.

This Act may be cited as the 'Economic Espionage Act of 1996'.

TITLE I--PROTECTION OF TRADE SECRETS

SEC. 101. PROTECTION OF TRADE SECRETS.

(a) IN GENERAL- Title 18, United States Code, is amended by inserting after chapter 89 the following:

CHAPTER 90--PROTECTION OF TRADE SECRETS

`Sec.

`1831. Economic espionage.

`1832. Theft of trade secrets.

`1833. Exceptions to prohibitions.

`1834. Criminal forfeiture.

`1835. Orders to preserve confidentiality.

`1836. Civil proceedings to enjoin violations.

`1837. Conduct outside the United States.

`1838. Construction with other laws.

`1839. Definitions.

`Sec. 1831. Economic espionage

`(a) IN GENERAL- Whoever, intending or knowing that the offense will benefit any foreign government, foreign instrumentality, or foreign agent, knowingly--

`(1) steals, or without authorization appropriates, takes, carries away, or conceals, or by fraud, artifice, or deception obtains a trade secret;

`(2) without authorization copies, duplicates, sketches, draws, photographs, downloads, uploads, alters, destroys, photocopies, replicates, transmits, delivers, sends, mails, communicates, or conveys a trade secret;

`(3) receives, buys, or possesses a trade secret, knowing the same to have been stolen or appropriated, obtained, or converted without authorization;

`(4) attempts to commit any offense described in any of paragraphs (1) through (3); or

`(5) conspires with one or more other persons to commit any offense described in any of paragraphs (1) through (3), and one or more of such persons do any act to effect the object of the conspiracy, shall, except as provided in subsection (b), be fined not more than $500,000 or imprisoned not more than 15 years, or both.

`(b) ORGANIZATIONS- Any organization that commits any offense described in subsection (a) shall be fined not more than $10,000,000.

`Sec. 1832. Theft of trade secrets

`(a) Whoever, with intent to convert a trade secret, that is related to or included in a product that is produced for or placed in interstate or foreign commerce, to the economic benefit of anyone other than the owner thereof, and intending or knowing that the offense will, injure any owner of that trade secret, knowingly--

`(1) steals, or without authorization appropriates, takes, carries away, or conceals, or by fraud, artifice, or deception obtains such information;

`(2) without authorization copies, duplicates, sketches, draws, photographs, downloads, uploads, alters, destroys, photocopies, replicates, transmits, delivers, sends, mails, communicates, or conveys such information;

`(3) receives, buys, or possesses such information, knowing the same to have been stolen or appropriated, obtained, or converted without authorization;

`(4) attempts to commit any offense described in paragraphs (1) through (3); or

`(5) conspires with one or more other persons to commit any offense described in paragraphs (1) through (3), and one or more of such persons do any act to effect the object of the conspiracy, shall, except as provided in subsection (b), be fined under this title or imprisoned not more than 10 years, or both.

`(b) Any organization that commits any offense described in subsection (a) shall be fined not more than $5,000,000.

`Sec. 1833. Exceptions to prohibitions

`This chapter does not prohibit--

`(1) any otherwise lawful activity conducted by a governmental entity of the United States, a State, or a political subdivision of a State; or

`(2) the reporting of a suspected violation of law to any governmental entity of the United States, a State, or a political subdivision of a State, if such entity has lawful authority with respect to that violation.

`Sec. 1834. Criminal forfeiture

`(a) The court, in imposing sentence on a person for a violation of this chapter, shall order, in addition to any other sentence imposed, that the person forfeit to the United States--

`(1) any property constituting, or derived from, any proceeds the person obtained, directly or indirectly, as the result of such violation; and

`(2) any of the person's property used, or intended to be used, in any manner or part, to commit or facilitate the commission of such violation, if the court in its discretion so determines, taking into consideration the nature, scope, and proportionality of the use of the property in the offense.

`(b) *Property subject to forfeiture under this section, any seizure and disposition thereof, and any administrative or judicial proceeding in relation thereto, shall be governed by section 413 of the Comprehensive Drug Abuse Prevention and Control Act of 1970 (21 U.S.C. 853), except for subsections (d) and (j) of such section, which shall not apply to forfeitures under this section.*

`*Sec. 1835. Orders to preserve confidentiality*

`*In any prosecution or other proceeding under this chapter, the court shall enter such orders and take such other action as may be necessary and appropriate to preserve the confidentiality of trade secrets, consistent with the requirements of the Federal Rules of Criminal and Civil Procedure, the Federal Rules of Evidence, and all other applicable laws. An interlocutory appeal by the United States shall lie from a decision or order of a district court authorizing or directing the disclosure of any trade secret.*

`*Sec. 1836. Civil proceedings to enjoin violations*

`(a) *The Attorney General may, in a civil action, obtain appropriate injunctive relief against any violation of this section.*

`(b) *The district courts of the United States shall have exclusive original jurisdiction of civil actions under this subsection.*

`*Sec. 1837. Applicability to conduct outside the United States*

`*This chapter also applies to conduct occurring outside the United States if--*

`(1) *the offender is a natural person who is a citizen or permanent resident alien of the United States, or an organization organized under the laws of the United States or a State or political subdivision thereof; or*

`(2) *an act in furtherance of the offense was committed in the United States.*

`*Sec. 1838. Construction with other laws*

`*This chapter shall not be construed to preempt or displace any other remedies, whether civil or criminal, provided by United States Federal, State, commonwealth, possession, or territory law for the misappropriation of a trade secret, or to affect the otherwise lawful disclosure of information by any Government employee under section 552 of title 5 (commonly known as the Freedom of Information Act).*

`*Sec. 1839. Definitions*

`*As used in this chapter--*

`(1) *the term 'foreign instrumentality' means any agency, bureau, ministry, component, institution, association, or any legal, commercial, or business organization, corporation, firm, or entity that is substantially owned, controlled, sponsored, commanded, managed, or dominated by a foreign government;*

`(2) *the term `foreign agent' means any officer, employee, proxy, servant, delegate, or representative of a foreign government;*

`(3) *the term 'trade secret' means all forms and types of financial, business, scientific, technical, economic, or engineering information, including patterns, plans,* compilations, program devices, formulas, designs, prototypes, methods, tech-niques, processes, procedures, programs, or codes, whether tangible or intangible, and whether or how stored, compiled, or memorialized physically, electronically, graphically, photographically, or in writing if--

`(A) the owner thereof has taken reasonable measures to keep such informa-tion secret; and

`(B) the information derives independent economic value, actual or potential, from not being generally known to, and not being readily ascertainable through proper means by, the public; and

`(4) the term `owner', with respect to a trade secret, means the person or entity in whom or in which rightful legal or equitable title to, or license in, the trade secret is reposed.

(b) CLERICAL AMENDMENT- The table of chapters at the beginning part I of title 18, United States Code, is amended by inserting after the item relating to chapter 89 the following:

1831'.

(c) REPORTS- Not later than 2 years and 4 years after the date of the enactment of this Act, the Attorney General shall report to Congress on the amounts received and distributed from fines for offenses under this chapter deposited in the Crime Victims Fund established by section 1402 of the Victims of Crime Act of 1984 (42 U.S.C. 10601).

APPENDIX C
Uniform Trade Secrets Act

SECTION 1. DEFINITIONS

As used in this [Act], unless the context requires otherwise:

(1) *"Improper means" includes theft, bribery, misrepresentation, breach or inducement of a breach of a duty to maintain secrecy, or espionage through electronic or other means;*

(2) *"Misappropriation" means:*

(i) *acquisition of a trade secret of another by a person who knows or has reason to know that the trade secret was acquired by improper means; or*

(I) disclosure or use of a trade secret of another without express or implied consent by a person who

(A) *used improper means to acquire knowledge of the trade secret; or*

(B) *at the time of disclosure or use, knew or had reason to know that his knowledge of the trade secret was*

(I) derived from or through a person who had utilized improper means to acquire it;

(II) acquired under circumstances giving rise to a duty to maintain its secrecy or limit its use; or

(III) derived from or through a person who owed a duty to the person seeking relief to maintain its secrecy or limit its use; or

(C) *before a material change of his [or her] position, knew or had reason to know that it was a trade secret and that knowledge of it had been acquired by accident or mistake.*

(3) *"Person" means a natural person, corporation, business trust, estate, trust, partnership, association, joint venture, government, governmental subdivision or agency, or any other legal or commercial entity.*

(4) *"Trade secret" means information, including a formula, pattern, compilation, program, device, method, technique, or process, that:*

(i) *derives independent economic value, actual or potential, from not being generally known to, and not being readily ascertainable by proper means by, other persons who can obtain economic value from its disclosure or use, and*

(ii) *is the subject of efforts that are reasonable under the circumstances to maintain its secrecy.*

Comment

One of the broadly stated policies behind trade secret law is "the maintenance of standards of commercial ethics." Kewanee Oil Co. v. Bicron Corp., 416 U.S. 470 (1974). The Restatement of Torts, Section 757, Comment (f), notes: "A complete catalogue of improper means is not possible," but Section 1(1) includes a partial listing.

Proper means include:

1. Discovery by independent invention;

2. Discovery by "reverse engineering", that is, by starting with the known product and working backward to find the method by which it was developed. The acquisition of the known product must, of course, also be by a fair and honest means, such as purchase of the item on the open market for reverse engineering to be lawful;

3. Discovery under a license from the owner of the trade secret;

4. Observation of the item in public use or on public display;

5. Obtaining the trade secret from published literature.

Improper means could include otherwise lawful conduct which is improper under the circumstances; e.g., an airplane overflight used as aerial reconnaissance to determine the competitor's plant layout during construction of the plant. E. I. du Pont de Nemours & Co., Inc. v. Christopher, 431 F.2d 1012 (CA5, 1970), cert. den. 400 U.S. 1024 (1970). Because the trade secret can be destroyed through public knowledge, the unauthorized disclosure of a trade secret is also a misappropriation.

The type of accident or mistake that can result in a misappropriation under Section 1(2)(ii)(C) involves conduct by a person seeking relief that does not constitute a failure of efforts that are reasonable under the circumstances to maintain its secrecy under Section 1(4)(ii).

The definition of "trade secret" contains a reasonable departure from the Restatement of Torts (First) definition which required that a trade secret be "continuously used in one's business." The broader definition in the proposed Act extends protection to a plaintiff who has not yet had an opportunity or acquired the means to put a trade secret to use. The definition includes information that has commercial value from a negative viewpoint, for example the results of lengthy and expensive research which proves that a certain process will **not** work could be of great value to a competitor.

Cf. Telex Corp. v. IBM Corp., 510 F.2d 894 (CA10, 1975) per curiam, cert. dismissed 423 U.S. 802 (1975) (liability imposed for developmental cost savings *with respect to product not marketed). Because a trade secret need not be exclusive to confer a competitive advantage, different independent developers can acquire rights in the same trade secret.*

The words "method, technique" are intended to include the concept of "know-how."

The language "not being generally known to and not being readily ascertainable by proper means by other persons" does not require that information be generally known to the public for trade secret rights to be lost. If the principal ~~person~~ persons *who can obtain economic benefit from information* ~~is~~ are *aware of it, there is no trade secret. A method of casting metal, for example, may be unknown to the general public but readily known within the foundry industry.*

Information is readily ascertainable if it is available in trade journals, reference books, or published materials. Often, the nature of a product lends itself to being readily copied as soon as it is available on the market. On the other hand, if reverse engineering is lengthy and expensive, a person who discovers the trade secret through reverse engineering can have a trade secret in the information obtained from reverse engineering.

Finally, reasonable efforts to maintain secrecy have been held to include advising employees of the existence of a trade secret, limiting access to a trade secret on "need to know basis", and controlling plant access. On the other hand, public disclosure of information through display, trade journal publications, advertising, or other carelessness can preclude protection.

The efforts required to maintain secrecy are those "reasonable under the circumstances." The courts do not require that extreme and unduly expensive procedures be taken to protect trade secrets against flagrant industrial espionage. See E. I. du Pont de Nemours & Co., Inc. v. Christopher, supra. It follows that reasonable use of a trade secret including controlled disclosure to employees and licensees is consistent with the requirement of relative secrecy.

SECTION 2. INJUNCTIVE RELIEF

(a) *Actual or threatened misappropriation may be enjoined. Upon application to the court, an injunction shall be terminated when the trade secret has ceased to exist, but the injunction may be continued for an additional reasonable period of time in order to eliminate commercial advantage that otherwise would be derived from the misappropriation.*

(b) ~~*If the court determines that it would be unreasonable to prohibit future use*~~ In exceptional circumstances, *an injunction may condition future use upon payment of a reasonable royalty for no longer than the period of time* ~~the~~ for which *use could have been prohibited. Exceptional circumstances include, but are not limited to, a material and prejudicial change of position prior to acquiring knowledge or reason to know of misappropriation that renders a prohibitive injunction inequitable.*

(c) *In appropriate circumstances, affirmative acts to protect a trade secret may be compelled by court order.*

Comment

Injunctions restraining future use and disclosure of misappropriated trade secrets frequently are sought. Although punitive perpetual injunctions have been granted, e.g., Elcor Chemical Corp. v. Agri-Sul, Inc., 494 S.W.2d 204 (Tex.Civ.App.1973), Section 2(a) of this Act adopts the position of the trend of authority limiting the duration of injunctive relief to the extent of the temporal advantage over good faith competitors gained by a misappropriator. See, e.g., K-2 Ski Co. v. Head Ski Co., Inc., 506 F.2d 471 (CA9, 1974) (maximum appropriate duration of both temporary and permanent injunctive relief is period of time it would have taken defendant to discover trade secrets lawfully through either independent development or reverse engineering of plaintiff's products).

The general principle of Section 2(a) and (b) is that an injunction should last for as long as is necessary, but no longer than is necessary, to eliminate the commercial advantage or "lead time" with respect to good faith competitors that a person has obtained through misappropriation. Subject to any additional period of restraint necessary to negate lead time, an injunction accordingly should terminate when a former trade secret becomes either generally known to good faith competitors or generally knowable to them because of the lawful availability of products that can be reverse engineered to reveal a trade secret.

For example, assume that A has a valuable trade secret of which B and C, the other industry members, are originally unaware. If B subsequently misappropriates the trade secret and is enjoined from use, but C later lawfully reverse engineers the trade secret, the injunction restraining B is subject to termination as soon as B's lead time has been dissipated. All of the persons who could derive economic value from use of the information are now aware of it, and there is no longer a trade secret under Section 1(4). It would be anti-competitive to continue to restrain B after any lead time that B had derived from misappropriation had been removed.

If a misappropriator either has not taken advantage of lead time or good faith competitors already have caught up with a misappropriator at the time that a case is decided, future disclosure and use of a former trade secret by a misappropriator will not damage a trade secret owner and no injunctive restraint of future disclosure and use is appropriate. See, e.g., Northern Petrochemical Co. v. Tomlinson, 484 F.2d 1057 (CA7, 1973) (affirming trial court's denial of preliminary injunction in part because an explosion at its plant prevented an alleged misappropriator from taking advantage of lead time); Kubik, Inc. v. Hull, 185 USPQ 391 (Mich.App.1974) (discoverability of trade secret by lawful reverse engineering made by injunctive relief punitive rather than compensatory).

Section 2(b) deals with ~~a distinguishable~~ *the special situation in which future use by a misappropriator will damage a trade secret owner but an injunction against future use nevertheless is* ~~unreasonable under the particular~~ inappropriate due to exceptional *circumstances* ~~of a case. Situations in which this unreasonableness can exist~~ Exceptional circumstances *include the existence of an overriding public interest which requires the denial of a prohibitory injunction against future damaging use and a person's reasonable reliance upon acquisition of a misappropriated trade secret in good faith and without reason to know of its prior misappropriation that would be prejudiced by a prohibitory injunction against future damaging use. Republic Aviation Corp. v. Schenk, 152 USPQ 830 (N.Y.Sup.Ct.1967) illustrates the public interest justification for withholding prohibitory injunctive relief. The court considered that enjoining a misappropriator from supplying the U.S. with an aircraft weapons control system would have endangered military personnel in Viet Nam. The prejudice to a good faith third party justification for withholding prohibitory injunctive relief can arise upon a trade secret owner's notification to a good faith third party that the third party has knowledge of a trade secret as a result of misappropriation by another. This notice suffices to make the third party a misappropriator thereafter under Section 1(2)(ii)(B)(I). In weighing an aggrieved person's interests and the interests of a third party who has relied in good faith upon his or her ability to utilize information, a court may conclude that restraining future use of the information by the third party is unwarranted. With respect to innocent acquirers of misappropriated trade secrets, Section 2(b) is consistent with the principle of 4 Restatement Torts (First) § 758(b) (1939), but rejects the Restatement's literal conferral of absolute immunity upon all third parties who have paid value in good faith for a trade secret misappropriated by another. The position taken by the Uniform Act is supported by Forest Laboratories, Inc. v. Pillsbury Co., 452 F.2d 621 (CA7, 1971) in which a defendant's purchase of assets of a corporation to which a trade secret had been disclosed in confidence was not considered to confer immunity upon the defendant.*

When Section 2(b) applies, a court ~~is given~~ has discretion to substitute an *injunction conditioning future use upon payment of a reasonable royalty for an injunction prohibiting future use. Like all injunctive relief for misappropriation, a royalty order injunction is appropriate only if a misappropriator has obtained a competitive advantage through misappropriation and only for the duration of that competitive advantage. In some situations, typically those involving good faith acquirers of trade secrets misappropriated by others, a court may conclude that the same considerations that render a prohibitory injunction against future use inappropriate also render a royalty order injunction inappropriate. See, generally, Prince Manufacturing, Inc. v. Automatic Partner, Inc., 198 USPQ 618 (N.J.Super. Ct.1976) (purchaser of misappropriator's assets from receiver after trade secret disclosed to public through sale of product not subject to liability for misappropriation).*

A royalty order injunction under Section 2(b) should be distinguished from a reasonable royalty alternative measure of damages under Section 3(a). See the Comment to Section 3 for discussion of the differences in the remedies.

Section 2(c) authorizes mandatory injunctions requiring that a misappropriator return the fruits of misappropriation to an aggrieved person, e.g., the return of stolen blueprints or the surrender of surreptitious photographs or recordings.

Where more than one person is entitled to trade secret protection with respect to the same information, only that one from whom misappropriation occurred is entitled to a remedy.

SECTION 3. DAMAGES

(a) ~~In addition to or in lieu of injunctive relief~~ *Except to the extent that a material and prejudicial change of position prior to acquiring knowledge or reason to know of misappropriation renders a monetary recovery inequitable, a complainant* ~~may~~ *is entitled to recover damages for* ~~the actual loss caused by~~ *misappropriation. A* ~~complainant also may recover for~~ *Damages can include both the actual loss caused by misappropriation and the unjust enrichment caused by misappropriation that is not taken into account in computing* ~~damages for~~ *actual loss. In lieu of damages measured by any other methods, the damages caused by misappropriation may be measured by imposition of liability for a reasonable royalty for a misappropriator's unauthorized disclosure or use of a trade secret.*

(b) *If willful and malicious misappropriation exists, the court may award exemplary damages in an amount not exceeding twice any award made under subsection (a).*

Comment

Like injunctive relief, a monetary recovery for trade secret misappropriation is appropriate only for the period in which information is entitled to protection as a trade secret, plus the additional period, if any, in which a misappropriator retains an advantage over good faith competitors because of misappropriation. Actual damage to a complainant and unjust benefit to a misappropriator are caused by misappropriation during this time alone. See Conmar Products Corp. v. Universal Slide Fastener Co., 172 F.2d 150 (CA2, 1949) (no remedy for period subsequent to disclosure of trade secret by issued patent); Carboline Co. v. Jarboe, 454 S.W.2d 540 (Mo.1970) (recoverable monetary relief limited to period that it would have taken misappropriator to discover trade secret without misappropriation). A claim for actual damages and net profits can be combined with a claim for injunctive relief, but, if both claims are granted, the injunctive relief ordinarily will preclude a monetary award for a period in which the injunction is effective.

As long as there is no double counting, Section 3(a) adopts the principle of the recent cases allowing recovery of both a complainant's actual losses and a misappropriator's unjust benefit that are caused by misappropriation. E.g., Tri-Tron International v. Velto, 525 F.2d 432 (CA9, 1975) (complainant's loss and misappropriator's benefit can be combined). Because certain cases may have sanctioned double counting in a combined award of losses and unjust benefit, e.g., Telex Corp. v. IBM Corp., 510 F.2d 894 (CA10, 1975) (per curiam), cert. dismissed, 423 U.S. 802 (1975) (IBM recovered rentals lost due to displacement by misappropriator's products without deduction for expenses saved by displacement; as a result of rough approximations adopted by the trial judge, IBM also may have recovered developmental costs saved by misappropriator through misappropriation with respect to the same customers), the Act adopts an express prohibition upon the counting of the same item as both a loss to a complainant and an unjust benefit to a misappropriator.

As an alternative to all other methods of measuring damages caused by a misappropriator's past conduct, a complainant can request that damages be based upon a demonstrably reasonable royalty for a misappropriator's unauthorized disclosure or use of a trade secret. In order to justify this alternative measure of damages, there must be competent evidence of the amount of a reasonable royalty.

The reasonable royalty alternative measure of damages for a misappropriator's past conduct under Section 3(a) is readily distinguishable from a Section 2(b) royalty order injunction, which conditions a misappropriator's future ability to use a trade secret upon payment of a reasonable royalty. A Section 2(b) royalty order injunction is appropriate only in exceptional circumstances; whereas a reasonable royalty measure of damages is a general option. Because Section 3(a) damages are awarded for a misappropriator's past conduct and a Section 2(b) royalty order injunction regulates a misappropriator's future conduct, both remedies cannot be awarded for the same conduct. If a royalty order injunction is appropriate because of a person's material and prejudicial change of position prior to having reason to know that a trade secret has been acquired from a misappropriator, damages, moreover, should not be awarded for past conduct that occurred prior to notice that a misappropriated trade secret has been acquired.

Monetary relief can be appropriate whether or not injunctive relief is granted under Section 2. If a person charged with misappropriation has ~~acquired~~ *materially and prejudicially changed position in reliance upon* knowledge of a trade secret *acquired* in good faith *and* without reason to know of its misappropriation by another, however, the same considerations that can justify denial of all injunctive relief also can justify denial of all monetary relief. See Conmar Products Corp. v. Universal Slide Fastener Co., 172 F.2d 1950 (CA2, 1949) (no relief against new employer of employee subject to contractual obligation not to disclose former employer's trade secrets where new employer innocently had committed $40,000 to develop the trade secrets prior to notice of misappropriation).

If willful and malicious misappropriation is found to exist, Section 3(b) authorizes the court to award a complainant exemplary damages in addition to the actual recovery under Section 3(a) an amount not exceeding twice that recovery. This provision follows federal patent law in leaving discretionary trebling to the judge even though there may be a jury, compare 35 U.S.C. Section 284 (1976).

Whenever more than one person is entitled to trade secret protection with respect to the same information, only that one from whom misappropriation occurred is entitled to a remedy.

SECTION 4. ATTORNEY'S FEES

If (i) a claim of misappropriation is made in bad faith, (ii) a motion to terminate an injunction is made or resisted in bad faith, or (iii) willful and malicious misappropriation exists, the court may award reasonable attorney's fees to the prevailing party.

Comment

Section 4 allows a court to award reasonable attorney fees to a prevailing party in specified circumstances as a deterrent to specious claims of misappropriation, to specious efforts by a misappropriator to terminate injunctive relief, and to willful and malicious misappropriation. In the latter situation, the court should take into consideration the extent to which a complainant will recover exemplary damages in determining whether additional attorney's fees should be awarded. Again, patent law is followed in allowing the judge to determine whether attorney's fees should be awarded even if there is a jury, compare 35 U.S.C. Section 285 (1976).

SECTION 5. PRESERVATION OF SECRECY

In an action under this [Act], a court shall preserve the secrecy of an alleged trade secret by reasonable means, which may include granting protective orders in connection with discovery proceedings, holding in-camera hearings, sealing the records of the action, and ordering any person involved in the litigation not to disclose an alleged trade secret without prior court approval.

Comment

If reasonable assurances of maintenance of secrecy could not be given, meritorious trade secret litigation would be chilled. In fashioning safeguards of confidentiality, a court must ensure that a respondent is provided sufficient information to present a defense and a trier of fact sufficient information to resolve the merits. In addition to the illustrative techniques specified in the statute, courts have protected secrecy in these cases by restricting disclosures to a party's counsel and his or her assistants and by appointing a disinterested expert as a special master to hear secret information and report conclusions to the court.

SECTION 6. STATUTE OF LIMITATIONS

An action for misappropriation must be brought within 3 years after the misappropriation is discovered or by the exercise of reasonable diligence should have been discovered. For the purposes of this section, a continuing misappropriation constitutes a single claim.

Comment

There presently is a conflict of authority as to whether trade secret misappropriation is a continuing wrong. Compare Monolith Portland Midwest Co. v. Kaiser Aluminum & Chemical Corp., 407 F.2d 288 (CA9, 1969) (no not a continuing wrong under California law – limitation period upon all recovery begins upon initial misappropriation) with Underwater Storage, Inc. v. U. S. Rubber Co., 371 F.2d 950 (CADC, 1966), cert. den., 386 U.S. 911 (1967) (continuing wrong under general principles – limitation period with respect to a specific act of misappropriation begins at the time that the act of misappropriation occurs).

This Act rejects a continuing wrong approach to the statute of limitations but delays the commencement of the limitation period until an aggrieved person discovers or reasonably should have discovered the existence of misappropriation.

123

If objectively reasonable notice of misappropriation exists, three years is sufficient time to vindicate one's legal rights.

SECTION 7. EFFECT ON OTHER LAW.

(a) ~~This~~ *Except as provided in subsection (b), this* [Act] displaces conflicting tort, restitutionary, and other law of this State ~~pertaining to~~ *providing* civil ~~liability~~ *remedies* for misappropriation of a trade secret.
   (b) This [Act] does not affect:
   (1) contractual ~~or other civil liability or relief that is~~ *remedies, whether or* not based upon misappropriation of a trade secret; ~~or~~
   (2) ~~criminal liability for~~ *other civil remedies that are not based upon* misappropriation of a trade secret.; *or*
   (3) *criminal remedies, whether or not based upon misappropriation of a trade secret.*

Comment

This Act ~~is not a comprehensive remedy~~ does not deal with criminal remedies for trade secret misappropriation and is not a comprehensive statement of civil remedies. It applies to ~~duties imposed by law in order~~ a duty to protect competitively significant secret information that is imposed by law. It does not apply to ~~duties~~ a duty voluntarily assumed through an express or an implied-in-fact contract. The enforceability of covenants not to disclose trade secrets and covenants not to compete that are intended to protect trade secrets, for example, ~~are~~ is governed by other law. The Act also does not apply to ~~duties~~ a duty imposed by law that ~~are~~ is not dependent upon the existence of competitively significant secret information, like an agent's duty of loyalty to his or her principal.

SECTION 8. UNIFORMITY OF APPLICATION AND CONSTRUCTION

This [Act] shall be applied and construed to effectuate its general purpose to make uniform the law with respect to the subject of this [Act] among states enacting it.

SECTION 9. SHORT TITLE

This [Act] may be cited as the Uniform Trade Secrets Act.

SECTION 10. SEVERABILITY

If any provision of this [Act] or its application to any person or circumstances is held invalid, the invalidity does not affect other provisions or applications of the [Act] which can be given effect without the invalid provision or application, and to this end the provisions of this [Act] are severable.

SECTION 11. TIME OF TAKING EFFECT

This [Act] takes effect on and does not apply to misappropriation occurring prior to the effective date. With respect to a continuing misappropriation that began prior to the effective date, the [Act] also does not apply to the continuing misappropriation that occurs after the effective date.

Comment

The Act applies exclusively to misappropriation that begins after its effective date. Neither misappropriation that began and ended before the effective date nor misappropriation that began before the effective date and continued thereafter is subject to the Act.

APPENDIX D
Homeland Security Act of 2002

Homeland Security Act of 2002 – **Title I: Department of Homeland Security** – (Sec. 101) Establishes a Department of Homeland Security (DHS) as an executive department of the United States, headed by a Secretary of Homeland Security (Secretary) appointed by the President, by and with the advice and consent of the Senate, to: (1) prevent terrorist attacks within the United States; (2) reduce the vulnerability of the United States to terrorism; (3) minimize the damage, and assist in the recovery, from terrorist attacks that occur within the United States; (4) carry out all functions of entities transferred to DHS; (5) ensure that the functions of the agencies and subdivisions within DHS that are not related directly to securing the homeland are not diminished or neglected except by a specific Act of Congress; (6) ensure that the overall economic security of the United States is not diminished by efforts, activities, and programs aimed at securing the homeland; and (7) monitor connections between illegal drug trafficking and terrorism, coordinate efforts to sever such connections, and otherwise contribute to efforts to interdict illegal drug trafficking. Vests primary responsibility for investigating and prosecuting acts of terrorism in Federal, State, and local law enforcement agencies with proper jurisdiction except as specifically provided by law with respect to entities transferred to DHS under this Act.

(Sec. 102) Directs the Secretary to appoint a Special Assistant to carry out specified homeland security liaison activities between DHS and the private sector.

(Sec. 103) Creates the following: (1) a Deputy Secretary of Homeland Security; (2) an Under Secretary for Information Analysis and Infrastructure Protection; (3) an Under Secretary for Science and Technology; (4) an Under Secretary for Border and Transportation Security; (5) an Under Secretary for Emergency Preparedness and Response; (6) a Director of the Bureau of Citizenship and Immigration Services; (7) an Under Secretary for Management; (8) not more than 12 Assistant Secretaries; and (9) a General Counsel. Establishes an Inspector General (to be appointed under the Inspector General Act of 1978). Requires the following individuals to assist the Secretary in the performance of the Secretary's functions: (1) the Commandant of the Coast Guard; (2) the Director of the Secret Service; (3) a Chief Information Officer; (4) a Chief Human Capital Officer; (5) a Chief Financial Officer; and (6) an Officer for Civil Rights and Civil Liberties.

Title II: Information Analysis and Infrastructure Protection – Subtitle A: Directorate for Information Analysis and Infrastructure Protection; Access to Information – (Sec. 201) Establishes in the Department: (1) a Directorate for Information Analysis and Infrastructure Protection, headed by an Under Secretary for Information Analysis and Infrastructure Protection; (2) an Assistant Secretary for Information Analysis; and (3) an Assistant Secretary for Infrastructure Protection.

Requires the Under Secretary to: (1) access, receive, and analyze law enforcement and intelligence information from Federal, State, and local agencies and the private sector to identify the nature, scope, and identity of terrorist threats to the United States, as well as potential U.S. vulnerabilities; (2) carry out comprehensive assessments of vulnerabilities of key U.S. resources and critical infrastructures; (3) integrate relevant information, analyses, and vulnerability assessments to identify protection priorities; (4) ensure timely and efficient Department access to necessary information for discharging responsibilities; (5) develop a comprehensive national plan for securing key U.S. resources and critical infrastructures; (6) recommend necessary measures to protect such resources and infrastructure in coordination with other entities; (7) administer the Homeland Security Advisory System; (8) review, analyze, and make recommendations for improvements in policies and procedures governing the sharing of law enforcement, intelligence, and intelligence-related information and other information related to homeland security within the Federal Government and between the Federal Government and State and local government agencies and authorities; (9) disseminate Department homeland security information to other appropriate Federal, State, and local agencies; (10) consult with the Director of Central Intelligence (DCI) and other appropriate Federal intelligence, law enforcement, or other elements to establish collection priorities and strategies for information relating the terrorism threats; (11) consult with State and local governments and private entities to ensure appropriate exchanges of information relating to such threats; (12) ensure the protection from unauthorized disclosure of homeland security and intelligence information; (13) request additional information from appropriate entities relating to threats of terrorism in the United States; (14) establish and utilize a secure communications and information technology infrastructure for receiving and analyzing data;

(15) ensure the compatibility and privacy protection of shared information databases and analytical tools; (16) coordinate training and other support to facilitate the identification and sharing of information; (17) coordinate activities with elements of the intelligence community, Federal, State, and local law enforcement agencies, and the private sector; and (18) provide intelligence and information analysis and support to other elements of the Department. Provides for: (1) staffing, including the use of private sector analysts; and (2) cooperative agreements for the detail of appropriate personnel.

Transfers to the Secretary the functions, personnel, assets, and liabilities of the following entities: (1) the National Infrastructure Protection Center of the Federal Bureau of Investigation (other than the Computer Investigations and Operations Section); (2) the National Communications System of the Department of Defense; (3) the Critical Infrastructure Assurance Offices of the Department of Commerce; (4) the National Infrastructure Simulation and Analysis Center of the Department of Energy and its energy security and assurance program; and (5) the Federal Computer Incident Response Center of the General Services Administration.

Amends the National Security Act of 1947 to include as elements of the intelligence community the Department elements concerned with analyses of foreign intelligence information.

(Sec. 202) Gives the Secretary access to all reports, assessments, analyses, and unevaluated intelligence relating to threats of terrorism against the United States, and to all information concerning infrastructure or other vulnerabilities to terrorism, whether or not such information has been analyzed. Requires all Federal agencies to promptly provide to the Secretary: (1) all reports, assessments, and analytical information relating to such threats and to other areas of responsibility assigned to the Secretary; (2) all information concerning the vulnerability of U.S. infrastructure or other U.S. vulnerabilities to terrorism, whether or not it has been analyzed; (3) all other information relating to significant and credible threats of terrorism, whether or not it has been analyzed; and (4) such other information or material as the President may direct. Requires the Secretary to be provided with certain terrorism-related information from law enforcement agencies that is currently required to be provided to the DCI.

Subtitle B: Critical Infrastructure Information – Critical Infrastructure Information Act of 2002 – (Sec. 213) Allows a critical infrastructure protection program to be so designated by either the President or the Secretary.

(Sec. 214) Exempts from the Freedom of Information Act and other Federal and State disclosure requirements any critical infrastructure information that is voluntarily submitted to a covered Federal agency for use in the security of critical infrastructure and protected systems, analysis, warning, interdependency study, recovery, reconstitution, or other informational purpose when accompanied by an express statement that such information is being submitted voluntarily in expectation of such nondisclosure protection. Requires the Secretary to establish specified procedures for the receipt, care, and storage by Federal agencies of critical infrastructure information voluntarily submitted. Provides criminal penalties for the unauthorized disclosure of such information.

Authorizes the Federal Government to issue advisories, alerts, and warnings to relevant companies, targeted sectors, other governmental entities, or the general public regarding potential threats to critical infrastructure.

Subtitle C: Information Security – (Sec. 221) Requires the Secretary to establish procedures on the use of shared information that: (1) limit its re-dissemination to ensure it is not used for an unauthorized purpose; (2) ensure its security and confidentiality; (3) protect the constitutional and statutory rights of individuals who are subjects of such information; and (4) provide data integrity through the timely removal and destruction of obsolete or erroneous names and information.

(Sec. 222) Directs the Secretary to appoint a senior Department official to assume primary responsibility for information privacy policy.

(Sec. 223) Directs the Under Secretary to provide: (1) to State and local government entities and, upon request, to private entities that own or operate critical information systems, analysis and warnings related to threats to and vulnerabilities of such systems, as well as crisis management support in response to threats to or attacks upon such systems; and (2) technical assistance, upon request, to private sector and other government entities with respect to emergency recovery plans to respond to major failures of such systems.

(Sec. 224) Authorizes the Under Secretary to establish a national technology guard (known as NET Guard) to assist local communities to respond to and recover from attacks on information systems and communications networks.

(Sec. 225) Cyber Security Enhancement Act of 2002 – Directs the U.S. Sentencing Commission to review and amend Federal sentencing guidelines and otherwise address crimes involving fraud in connection with computers and access to protected information, protected computers, or restricted data in interstate or foreign commerce or involving a computer used by or for the Federal Government. Requires a Commission report to Congress on actions taken and recommendations regarding statutory penalties for violations. Exempts from criminal penalties any disclosure made by an electronic communication service to a Federal, State, or local governmental entity if made in the good faith belief that an emergency involving danger of death or serious physical injury to any person requires disclosure without delay. Requires any government entity receiving such a disclosure to report it to the Attorney General.

Amends the Federal criminal code to: (1) prohibit the dissemination by electronic means of any such protected information; (2) increase criminal penalties for violations which cause death or serious bodily injury; (3) authorize the use by appropriate officials of emergency pen register and trap and trace devices in the case of either an immediate threat to a national security interest or an ongoing attack on a protected computer that constitutes a crime punishable by a prison term of greater than one year; (4) repeal provisions which provide a shorter term of imprisonment for certain offenses involving protection from the unauthorized interception and disclosure of wire, oral, or electronic communications; and (5) increase penalties for repeat offenses in connection with unlawful access to stored communications.

Subtitle D: Office of Science and Technology – (Sec. 231) Establishes within the Department of Justice (DOJ) an Office of Science and Technology whose mission is to: (1) serve as the national focal point for work on law enforcement technology (investigative and forensic technologies, corrections technologies, and technologies that support the judicial process); and (2) carry out programs that improve the safety and effectiveness of such technology and improve technology access by Federal, State, and local law enforcement agencies. Sets forth Office duties, including: (1) establishing and maintaining technology advisory groups and performance standards; (2) carrying out research, development, testing, evaluation, and cost-benefit analyses for improving the safety, effectiveness, and efficiency of technologies used by Federal, State, and local law enforcement agencies; and (3) operating the regional National Law Enforcement and Corrections Technology Centers (established under this Subtitle) and establishing additional centers. Requires the Office Director to report annually on Office activities.

(Sec. 234) Authorizes the Attorney General to transfer to the Office any other DOJ program or activity determined to be consistent with its mission. Requires a report from the Attorney General to the congressional judiciary committees on the implementation of this Subtitle.

131

(Sec. 235) Requires the Office Director to operate and support National Law Enforcement and Corrections Technology Centers and, to the extent necessary, establish new centers through a merit-based, competitive process. Requires such Centers to: (1) support research and development of law enforcement technology; (2) support the transfer and implementation of such technology; (3) assist in the development and dissemination of guidelines and technological standards; and (4) provide technology assistance, information, and support for law enforcement, corrections, and criminal justice purposes. Requires the Director to: (1) convene an annual meeting of such Centers; and (2) report to Congress assessing the effectiveness of the Centers and identifying the number of Centers necessary to meet the technology needs of Federal, State, and local law enforcement in the United States.

(Sec. 237) Amends the Omnibus Crime Control and Safe Streets Act of 1968 to require the National Institute of Justice to: (1) research and develop tools and technologies relating to prevention, detection, investigation, and prosecution of crime; and (2) support research, development, testing, training, and evaluation of tools and technology for Federal, State, and local law enforcement agencies.

Title III: Science and Technology in Support of Homeland Security – (Sec. 301) Establishes in DHS a Directorate of Science and Technology, headed by an Under Secretary for Science and Technology, to be responsible for: (1) advising the Secretary regarding research and development (R&D) efforts and priorities in support of DHS missions; (2) developing a national policy and strategic plan for, identifying priorities, goals, objectives and policies for, and coordinating the Federal Government's civilian efforts to identify and develop countermeasures to chemical, biological, radiological, nuclear, and other emerging terrorist threats; (3) supporting the Under Secretary for Information Analysis and Infrastructure Protection by assessing and testing homeland security vulnerabilities and possible threats; (4) conducting basic and applied R&D activities relevant to DHS elements, provided that such responsibility does not extend to human health-related R&D activities; (5) establishing priorities for directing, funding, and conducting national R&D and procurement of technology systems for preventing the importation of chemical, biological, radiological, nuclear, and related weapons and material and for detecting, preventing, protecting against, and responding to terrorist attacks; (6) establishing a system for transferring homeland security developments or technologies to Federal, State, and local government and private sector entities; (7) entering into agreements with the Department of Energy (DOE) regarding the use of the national laboratories or sites and support of the science and technology base at those facilities; (8) collaborating with the Secretary of Agriculture and the Attorney General in the regulation of certain biological agents and toxins as provided in the Agricultural Bioterrorism Protection Act of 2002; (9) collaborating with the Secretary of Health and Human Services and the Attorney General in determining new biological agents and toxins that shall be listed as select agents in the Code of Federal Regulations; (10) supporting U.S. leadership in science and technology; (11) establishing and administering the primary R&D activities of DHS; (12) coordinating and integrating all DHS R&D activities; (13) coordinating with other appropriate executive agencies in developing and carrying out the science and technology agenda of DHS to reduce duplication and identify unmet needs; and (14) developing and overseeing the administration of guidelines for merit review of R&D projects throughout DHS and for the dissemination of DHS research.

(Sec. 303) Transfers to the Secretary: (1) specified DOE functions, including functions related to chemical and biological national security programs, nuclear smuggling programs and activities within the proliferation detection program, the nuclear assessment program, designated life sciences activities of the biological and environmental research program related to microbial pathogens, the Environmental Measurements Laboratory, and the advanced scientific computing research program at Lawrence Livermore National Laboratory; and (2) the National Bio-Weapons Defense Analysis Center of DOD.

(Sec. 304) Requires the HHS Secretary, with respect to civilian human health-related R&D activities relating to HHS countermeasures for chemical, biological, radiological, and nuclear and other emerging terrorist threats, to: (1) set priorities, goals, objectives, and policies and develop a coordinated strategy for such activities in collaboration with the Secretary to ensure consistency with the national policy and strategic plan; and (2) collaborate with the Secretary in developing specific benchmarks and outcome measurements for evaluating progress toward achieving such priorities and goals.

Amends the Public Health Service Act to: (1) authorize the HHS Secretary to declare that an actual or potential bioterrorist incident or other public health emergency makes advisable the administration of a covered countermeasure against smallpox to a category or categories of individuals; (2) require the HHS Secretary to specify the substances to be considered countermeasures and the beginning and ending dates of the period of the declaration; and (3) deem a covered person to be an employee of the Public Health Service with respect to liability arising out of administration of such a countermeasure.

Extends liability to the United States (with an exception) with respect to claims arising out of an administration of a covered countermeasure to an individual only if: (1) the countermeasure was administered by a qualified person for the purpose of preventing or treating smallpox during the effective period; (2) the individual was within a covered category; or (3) the qualified person administering the countermeasure had reasonable grounds to believe that such individual was within such category. Provides for a rebuttable presumption of an administration within the scope of a declaration in the case where an individual who is not vaccinated contracts vaccinia. Makes the remedy against the United States provided under such Act exclusive of any other civil action or proceeding against a covered person for any claim or suit arising out of the administration of a covered countermeasure.

(Sec. 305) Authorizes the Secretary, acting through the Under Secretary, to establish or contract with one or more federally funded R&D centers to provide independent analysis of homeland security issues or to carry out other responsibilities under this Act.

(Sec. 306) Directs the President to notify the appropriate congressional committees of any proposed transfer of DOE life sciences activities.

(Sec. 307) Establishes the Homeland Security Advanced Research Projects Agency to be headed by a Director who shall be appointed by the Secretary and who shall report to the Under Secretary. Requires the Director to administer the Acceleration Fund for Research and Development of Homeland Security Technologies (established by this Act) to award competitive, merit-reviewed grants, cooperative agreements, or contracts to public or private entities to: (1) support basic and applied homeland security research to promote revolutionary changes in technologies that would promote homeland security; (2) advance the development, testing and evaluation, and deployment of critical homeland security technologies; and (3) accelerate the prototyping and deployment of technologies that would address homeland security vulnerabilities. Allows the Director to solicit proposals to address specific vulnerabilities. Requires the Director to periodically hold homeland security technology demonstrations to improve contact among technology developers, vendors, and acquisition personnel.

Authorizes appropriations to the Fund. Earmarks ten percent of such funds for each fiscal year through FY 2005 for the Under Secretary, through joint agreement with the Commandant of the Coast Guard, to carry out R&D of improved ports, waterways, and coastal security surveillance and perimeter protection capabilities to minimize the possibility that Coast Guard cutters, aircraft, helicopters, and personnel will be diverted from non-homeland security missions to the ports, waterways, and coastal security mission.

(Sec. 308) Requires the Secretary, acting through the Under Secretary, to: (1) operate extramural R&D programs to ensure that colleges, universities, private research institutes, and companies (and consortia thereof) from as many areas of the United States as practicable participate; and (2) establish a university-based center or centers for homeland security which shall establish a coordinated, university-based system to enhance the Nation's homeland security. Authorizes the Secretary, through the Under Secretary, to: (1) draw upon the expertise of any Government laboratory; and (2) establish a headquarters laboratory for DHS and additional laboratory units.

(Sec. 309) Allows the Secretary, in carrying out DHS missions, to utilize DOE national laboratories and sites through: (1) a joint sponsorship arrangement; (2) a direct contact between DHS and the applicable DOE laboratory or site; (3) any "work for others" basis made available by that laboratory or site; or (4) any other method provided by law. Allows DHS to be a joint sponsor: (1) with DOE of one or more DOE national laboratories; and (2) of a DOE site in the performance of work as if such site were a federally funded R&D center and the work were performed under a multiple agency sponsorship arrangement with DHS. Directs the Secretary and the Secretary of DOE to ensure that direct contracts between DHS and the operator of a DOE national laboratory or site for programs or activities transferred from DOE to DHS are separate from the direct contracts of DOE with such operator.

Establishes within the Directorate of Science and Technology an Office for National Laboratories which shall be responsible for the coordination and utilization of DOE national laboratories and sites in a manner to create a networked laboratory system to support DHS missions.

(Sec. 310) Directs the Secretary of Agriculture to transfer to the Secretary the Plum Island Animal Disease Center of the Department of Agriculture and provides for continued Department of Agriculture access to such Center.

(Sec. 311) Establishes within DHS a Homeland Security Science and Technology Advisory Committee to make recommendations with respect to the activities of the Under Secretary.

(Sec. 312) Directs the Secretary to establish the Homeland Security Institute, a federally funded R&D center. Includes among authorized duties for the Institute: (1) determination of the vulnerabilities of the Nation's critical infrastructures; (2) assessment of the costs and benefits of alternative approaches to enhancing security; and (3) evaluation of the effectiveness of measures deployed to enhance the security of institutions, facilities, and infrastructure that may be terrorist targets.

(Sec. 313) Requires the Secretary to establish and promote a program to encourage technological innovation in facilitating the mission of DHS, to include establishment of: (1) a centralized Federal clearinghouse to further the dissemination of information on technologies; and (2) a technical assistance team to assist in screening submitted proposals.

Title IV: Directorate of Border and Transportation Security – Subtitle A: Under Secretary for Border and Transportation Security – (Sec. 401) Establishes in DHS a Directorate of Border and Transportation Security to be headed by an Under Secretary for Border and Transportation Security. Makes the Secretary, acting through the Under Secretary for Border and Transportation Security, responsible for: (1) preventing the entry of terrorists and the instruments of terrorism into the United States; (2) securing the borders, territorial waters, ports, terminals, waterways, and air, land, and sea transportation systems of the United States; (3) carrying out the immigration enforcement functions vested by statute in, or performed by, the Commissioner of Immigration and Naturalization immediately before their transfer to the Under Secretary; (4) establishing and administering rules governing the granting of visas or other forms of permission to enter the United States to individuals who are not citizens or aliens lawfully admitted for permanent residence in the United States; (5) establishing national immigration enforcement policies and priorities; (6) administering the customs laws of the United States (with certain exceptions); (7) conducting the inspection and related administrative functions of the Department of Agriculture transferred to the Secretary; and (8) ensuring the speedy, orderly, and efficient flow of lawful traffic and commerce in carrying out the foregoing responsibilities.

(Sec. 403) Transfers to the Secretary the functions, personnel, assets, and liabilities of: (1) the U.S. Customs Service; (2) the Transportation Security Administration; (3) the Federal Protective Service of the General

Services Administration (GSA); (4) the Federal Law Enforcement Training Center of the Department of the Treasury; and (5) the Office for Domestic Preparedness of the Office of Justice Programs of the Department of Justice (DOJ).

Subtitle B: United States Customs Service – (Sec. 411) Establishes in DHS the U.S. Customs Service (transferred from the Department of the Treasury, but with certain customs revenue functions remaining with the Secretary of the Treasury). Authorizes the Secretary of the Treasury to appoint up to 20 new personnel to work with DHS personnel in performing customs revenue functions.

(Sec. 414) Requires the President to include a separate budget request for the U.S. Customs Service in the annual budget transmitted to Congress.

(Sec. 416) Directs the Comptroller General to report to Congress on all trade functions performed by the executive branch, specifying each agency that performs each such function.

(Sec. 417) Directs the Secretary to ensure that adequate staffing is provided to assure that levels of current customs revenue services will continue to be provided. Requires the Secretary to notify specified congressional committees prior to taking any action which would: (1) result in any significant reduction in customs revenue services (including hours of operation provided at any office within DHS or any port of entry); (2) eliminate or relocate any office of DHS which provides customs revenue services; or (3) eliminate any port of entry.

(Sec. 419) Amends the Consolidated Omnibus Budget Reconciliation Act of 1985 to create in the Treasury a separate Customs Commercial and Homeland Security Automation Account to contain merchandise processing (customs user) fees. Authorizes appropriations for FY 2003 through 2005 for establishment of the Automated Commercial Environment computer system for the processing of merchandise that is entered or released and for other purposes related to the functions of DHS.

Subtitle C: Miscellaneous Provisions – (Sec. 421) Transfers to the Secretary the functions of the Secretary of Agriculture relating to agricultural import and entry inspection activities under specified animal and plant protection laws.

Requires the Secretary of Agriculture and the Secretary to enter into an agreement to effectuate such transfer and to transfer periodically funds collected pursuant to fee authorities under the Food, Agriculture, Conservation, and Trade Act of 1990 to the Secretary for activities carried out by the Secretary for which such fees were collected.

Directs the Secretary of Agriculture to transfer to the Secretary not more than 3,200 full-time equivalent positions of the Department of Agriculture.

(Sec. 423) Directs the Secretary to establish a liaison office within DHS for the purpose of consulting with the Administrator of the Federal Aviation Administration before taking any action that might affect aviation safety, air carrier operations, aircraft airworthiness, or the use of airspace.

(Sec. 424) Requires the Transportation Security Administration to be maintained as a distinct entity within DHS under the Under Secretary for Border Transportation and Security for two years after enactment of this Act.

(Sec. 425) Amends Federal aviation law to require the Under Secretary of Transportation for Security to take certain action, if, in his discretion or at the request of an airport, he determines that the Transportation Security Administration is not able to deploy explosive detection systems at all airports required to have them by December 31, 2002. Requires the Under Secretary, in such circumstances, to: (1) submit to specified congressional committees a detailed plan for the deployment of explosive detection systems at such airport by December 31, 2003; and (2) take all necessary action to ensure that alternative means of screening all checked baggage is implemented.

(Sec. 426) Replaces the Secretary of Transportation with the Secretary of Homeland Security as chair of the Transportation Security Oversight Board. Requires the Secretary of Transportation to consult with the Secretary before approving airport development project grants relating to security equipment or the installation of bulk explosive detection systems.

(Sec. 427) Directs the Secretary, in coordination with the Secretary of Agriculture, the Secretary of Health and Human Services, and the head of each other department or agency determined to be appropriate by the Secretary, to ensure that appropriate information concerning inspections of articles that are imported or entered into the United States, and are inspected or regulated by one or more affected agencies, is timely and efficiently exchanged between the affected agencies. Requires the Secretary to report to Congress on the progress made in implementing this section.

(Sec. 428) Grants the Secretary exclusive authority to issue regulations with respect to, administer, and enforce the Immigration and Nationality Act (INA) and all other immigration and nationality laws relating to the functions of U.S. diplomatic and consular officers in connection with the granting or refusal of visas, and authority to refuse visas in accordance with law and to develop programs of homeland security training for consular officers, which authorities shall be exercised through the Secretary of State. Denies the Secretary authority, however, to alter or reverse the decision of a consular officer to refuse a visa to an alien.

Grants the Secretary authority also to confer or impose upon any U.S. officer or employee, with the consent of the head of the executive agency under whose jurisdiction such officer or employee is serving, any of these specified functions.

Authorizes the Secretary of State to direct a consular officer to refuse a visa to an alien if the Secretary of State deems such refusal necessary or advisable in the foreign policy or security interests of the United States.

Authorizes the Secretary to assign employees of DHS to any diplomatic and consular posts abroad to review individual visa applications and provide expert advice and training to consular officers regarding specific security threats relating to such applications and to conduct investigations with respect to matters under the Secretary's jurisdiction.

Directs the Secretary to study and report to Congress on the role of foreign nationals in the granting or refusal of visas and other documents authorizing entry of aliens into the United States.

Requires the Director of the Office of Science and Technology Policy to report to Congress on how the provisions of this section will affect procedures for the issuance of student visas.

Terminates after enactment of this Act all third party screening visa issuance programs in Saudi Arabia. Requires on-site personnel of DHS to review all visa applications prior to adjudication.

(Sec. 429) Requires visa denial information to be entered into the electronic data system as provided for in the Enhanced Border Security and Visa Entry Reform Act of 2002. Prohibits an alien denied a visa from being issued a subsequent visa unless the reviewing consular officer makes specified findings concerning waiver of ineligibility.

(Sec. 430) Establishes within the Directorate of Border and Transportation Security the Office for Domestic Preparedness to: (1) coordinate Federal preparedness for acts of terrorism, working with all State, local, tribal, county, parish, and private sector emergency response providers; (2) coordinate or consolidate systems of communications relating to homeland security at all levels of government; (3) direct and supervise Federal terrorism preparedness grant programs for all emergency response providers; and (4) perform specified other related duties.

Subtitle D: Immigration Enforcement Functions – (Sec. 441) Transfers from the Commissioner of Immigration and Naturalization to the Under Secretary for Border and Transportation Security all functions performed under the following programs, and all personnel, assets, and liabilities pertaining to such programs, immediately before such transfer occurs: (1) the Border Patrol program; (2) the detention and removal program; (3) the intelligence program; (4) the investigations program; and (5) the inspections program.

(Sec. 442) Establishes in the Department of Homeland Security (DHS) the Bureau of Border Security, headed by the Assistant Secretary of the Bureau of Border Security who shall: (1) report directly to the Under Secretary; (2) establish and oversee the policies for performing functions transferred to the Under Secretary and delegated to the Assistant Secretary by the Under Secretary; and (3) advise the Under Secretary with respect to any policy or operation of the Bureau that may affect the Bureau of Citizenship and Immigration Services.

Directs the Assistant Secretary to: (1) administer the program to collect information relating to nonimmigrant foreign students and other exchange program participants; and (2) implement a managerial rotation program.

Establishes the position of Chief of Policy and Strategy for the Bureau of Border Security, who shall: (1) make immigration enforcement policy recommendations; and (2) coordinate immigration policy issues with the Chief of Policy and Strategy for the Bureau of Citizenship and Immigration Services.

(Sec. 443) Makes the Under Secretary responsible for: (1) investigating noncriminal allegations of Bureau employee misconduct, corruption, and fraud that are not subject to investigation by the Inspector General for DHS; (2) inspecting and assessing Bureau operations; and (3) analyzing Bureau management.

(Sec. 444) Authorizes the Under Secretary to impose disciplinary action pursuant to policies and procedures applicable to FBI employees.

(Sec. 445) Requires the Secretary of Homeland Security to report on how the Bureau will enforce relevant INA provisions.

(Sec. 446) Expresses the sense of Congress that completing the 14-mile border fence project near San Diego, California, mandated by the Illegal Immigration Reform and Immigrant Responsibility Act of 1996 should be a priority for the Secretary.

Subtitle E: Citizenship and Immigration Services – (Sec. 451) Establishes in DHS a Bureau of Citizenship and Immigration Services, headed by the Director of the Bureau of Citizenship and Immigration Services, who shall: (1) establish the policies for performing and administering transferred functions; (2) establish national immigration services policies and priorities; and (3) implement a managerial rotation program.

Authorizes the Director to implement pilot initiatives to eliminate the backlog of immigration benefit applications.

Transfers all Immigration and Naturalization Service (INS) adjudications and related personnel and funding to the Director.

Establishes for the Bureau positions of: (1) Chief of Policy and Strategy; (2) legal adviser; (3) budget officer; and (4) Chief of the Office of Citizenship to promote citizenship instruction and training for aliens interested in becoming naturalized U.S. citizens.

(Sec. 452) Establishes within the DHS a Citizenship and Immigration Services Ombudsman, with local offices, to: (1) assist individuals and employers resolve problems with the Bureau; (2) identify problem areas; and (3) propose administrative and legislative changes.

(Sec. 453) Makes the Director responsible for (1) investigating non-criminal allegations of Bureau employee misconduct, corruption, and fraud that are not subject to investigation by the Inspector General of DHS; (2) inspecting and assessing Bureau operations; and (3) analyzing Bureau management.

(Sec. 454) Authorizes the Director to impose disciplinary action pursuant to policies and procedures applicable to FBI employees.

(Sec. 456) Sets forth transfer of authority and transfer and allocation of appropriations and personnel provisions.

(Sec. 457) Amends the INA to repeal the provision permitting fees for adjudication and naturalization services to be set at a level that will ensure recovery of the costs of similar services provided without charge to asylum applicants.

(Sec. 458) Amends the Immigration Services and Infrastructure Improvements Act of 2000 to change the deadline for the Attorney General to eliminate the backlog in the processing of immigration benefit applications to one year after enactment of this Act.

(Sec. 459) Directs the Secretary to report on how the Bureau of Citizenship and Immigration Services will efficiently complete transferred INS adjudications.

(Sec. 460) Directs the Attorney General to report on changes in law needed to ensure an appropriate response to emergent or unforseen immigration needs.

141

(Sec. 461) Directs the Secretary to: (1) establish an Internet-based system that will permit online information access to a person, employer, immigrant, or nonimmigrant about the processing status of any filings for any benefit under the INA; (2) conduct a feasibility study for online filing and improved processing; and (3) establish a Technology Advisory Committee.

(Sec. 462) Transfers to the Director of the Office of Refugee Resettlement of the Department of Health and Human Services (HHS) INS functions with respect to the care of unaccompanied alien children (as defined by this Act).

Sets forth the responsibilities of the Office for such children, including: (1) coordinating and implementing the care and placement of unaccompanied alien children who are in Federal custody, including appointment of independent legal counsel to represent the interests of each child; (2) identifying and overseeing individuals, entities, and facilities to house such children; (3) family reunification; (4) compiling, updating, and publishing at least annually a State-by-State list of professionals or other entities qualified to provide guardian and attorney representation services; (5) maintaining related biographical and statistical information; and (6) conducting investigations and inspections of residential facilities.

Directs the Office to: (1) consult with juvenile justice professionals to ensure such children's safety; and (2) not release such children upon their own recognizance.

Subtitle F: General Immigration Provisions – (Sec. 471) Abolishes INS upon completion of all transfers from it as provided for by this Act.

(Sec. 472) Authorizes the Attorney General and the Secretary to make voluntary separation incentive payments, after completion of a strategic restructuring plan, to employees of: (1) INS; (2) the Bureau of Border Security of DHS; and (3) the Bureau of Citizenship and Immigration Services of DHS.

(Sec. 473) Directs the Attorney General and the Secretary to conduct a demonstration project to determine whether policy or procedure revisions for employee discipline would result in improved personnel management.

(Sec. 474) Expresses the sense of Congress that: (1) the missions of the Bureau of Border Security and the Bureau of Citizenship and Immigration Services are equally important and should be adequately funded; and (2) the functions transferred should not operate at levels below those in effect prior to the enactment of this Act.

(Sec. 475) Establishes within the Office of Deputy Secretary a Director of Shared Services who shall be responsible for: (1) information resources management; and (2) records, forms, and file management.

(Sec. 476) Provides for budgetary and funding separation with respect to the Bureau of Citizenship and Immigration Services and the Bureau of Border Security.

(Sec. 477) Sets forth reporting and implementation plan provisions.

(Sec. 478) Directs the Secretary to annually report regarding: (1) the aggregate number of all immigration applications and petitions received, and processed; (2) regional statistics on the aggregate number of denied applications and petitions; (3) application and petition backlogs and a backlog elimination plan; (4) application and petition processing periods; (5) number, types, and disposition of grievances and plans to improve immigration services; and (6) appropriate use of immigration-related fees.

Expresses the sense of Congress that: (1) the quality and efficiency of immigration services should be improved after the transfers made by Act; and (2) the Secretary should undertake efforts to guarantee that such concerns are addressed after such effective date.

Title V: Emergency Preparedness and Response – (Sec. 501) Establishes in DHS a Directorate of Emergency Preparedness and Response, headed by an Under Secretary.

(Sec. 502) Requires the responsibilities of the Secretary, acting through the Under Secretary, to include: (1) helping to ensure the effectiveness of emergency response providers to terrorist attacks, major disasters, and other emergencies; (2) with respect to the Nuclear Incident Response Team, establishing and certifying compliance with standards, conducting joint and other exercises and training, and providing funds to the Department of Energy and the Environmental Protection Agency for homeland security planning, training, and equipment; (3) providing the Federal Government's response to terrorist attacks and major disasters; (4) aiding recovery from terrorist attacks and major disasters; (5) building a comprehensive national incident management system with Federal, State, and local governments to respond to such attacks and disasters; (6) consolidating existing Federal Government emergency response plans into a single, coordinated national response plan; and (7) developing comprehensive programs for developing interoperative communications technology and helping to ensure that emergency response providers acquire such technology.

(Sec. 503) Transfers to the Secretary the functions, personnel, assets, and liabilities of: (1) the Federal Emergency Management Agency (FEMA); (2) the Integrated Hazard Information System of the National Oceanic and Atmospheric Administration, which shall be renamed

FIRESAT; (3) the National Domestic Preparedness Office of the FBI; (4) the Domestic Emergency Support Teams of DOJ; (5) the Office of Emergency Preparedness, the National Disaster Medical System, and the Metropolitan Medical Response System of HHS; and (6) the Strategic National Stockpile of HHS.

(Sec. 504) Requires the Nuclear Incident Response Team, at the direction of the Secretary (in connection with an actual or threatened terrorist attack, major disaster, or other emergency in the United States), to operate as an organizational unit of DHS under the Secretary's authority and control.

(Sec. 505) Provides that, with respect to all public health-related activities to improve State, local, and hospital preparedness and response to chemical, biological, radiological, and nuclear and other emerging terrorist threats carried out by HHS (including the Public Health Service), the Secretary of HHS shall set priorities and preparedness goals and further develop a coordinated strategy for such activities in collaboration with the Secretary.

(Sec. 506) Defines the Nuclear Incident Response Team to include: (1) those entities of the Department of Energy that perform nuclear or radiological emergency support functions, radiation exposure functions at the medical assistance facility known as the Radiation Emergency Assistance Center/Training Site (REAC/TS), radiological assistance functions, and related functions; and (2) Environmental Protection Agency entities that perform such support functions and related functions.

(Sec. 507) Includes in the homeland security role of FEMA: (1) all functions and authorities prescribed by the Robert T. Stafford Disaster Relief and Emergency Assistance Act; and (2) a comprehensive, risk-based emergency management program of mitigation, of planning for building the emergency management profession, of response, of recovery, and of increased efficiencies. Maintains FEMA as the lead agency for the Federal Response Plan established under Executive Orders 12148 and 12656. Requires the FEMA Director to revise the Plan to reflect the establishment of and incorporate DHS.

(Sec. 508) Directs the Secretary, to the maximum extent practicable, to use national private sector networks and infrastructure for emergency response to major disasters.

(Sec. 509) Expresses the sense of Congress that the Secretary should: (1) use off-the-shelf commercially developed technologies to allow DHS to collect, manage, share, analyze, and disseminate information securely over multiple channels of communication; and (2) rely on commercial sources to supply goods and services needed by DHS.

Title VI: Treatment of Charitable Trusts for Members of the Armed Forces of the United States and Other Governmental Organizations – (Sec. 601) Sets forth requirements a charitable corporation, fund, foundation, or trust must meet to designate itself as a Johnny Micheal Spann Patriot Trust (a charitable trust for the spouses, dependents, and relatives of military and Federal personnel who lose their lives in the battle against terrorism that is named after the first American to die in such service following the September 11th terrorist attacks). Requires at least 85 percent of each Trust corpus to be distributed to such survivors and prohibits more than 15 percent from being used for administrative purposes. Prohibits: (1) any Trust activities from violating any prohibition against attempting to influence legislation; and (2) any such Trust from participating in any political campaign on behalf of a candidate for public office. Requires: (1) audits of each Trust that annually receives contributions of more than $1 million; and (2) Trust distributions to be made at least once a year. Provides for the notification of Trust beneficiaries.

Title VII: Management – (Sec. 701) Makes the Secretary, acting through the Under Secretary for Management, responsible for the management and administration of DHS. Details certain responsibilities of the Under Secretary with respect to immigration statistics. Transfers to the Under Secretary functions previously performed by the Statistics Branch of the Office of Policy and Planning of the Immigration and Naturalization Service (INS) with respect to: (1) the Border Patrol program; (2) the detention and removal program; (3) the intelligence program; (4) the investigations program; (5) the inspections program; and (6) INS adjudications.

(Sec. 702) Requires a chief financial officer, a chief information officer, and a chief human capital officer to report to the Secretary. Requires the chief human capital officer to ensure that all DHS employees are informed of their rights and remedies under merit system protection and principle provisions.

(Sec. 705) Requires the Secretary to appoint an Officer for Civil Rights and Civil Liberties who shall: (1) review and assess information alleging abuses of civil rights, civil liberties, and racial and ethnic profiling by employees and officials of DHS; and (2) make public information on the responsibilities and functions of, and how to contact, the Office.

(Sec. 706) Requires the Secretary to develop and submit to Congress a plan for consolidating and co-locating: (1) any regional offices or field offices of agencies that are transferred to DHS under this Act, if their officers are located in the same municipality; and (2) portions of regional and field offices of other Federal agencies, to the extent such offices perform functions that are transferred to the Secretary under this Act.

Title VIII: Coordination With Non-Federal Entities; Inspector General; United States Secret Service; Coast Guard; General Provisions – Subtitle A: Coordination with Non-Federal Entities – (Sec. 801) Establishes within the Office of the Secretary the Office for State and Local Government Coordination to oversee and coordinate Department homeland security programs for and relationships with State and local governments.

Subtitle B: Inspector General – (Sec. 811) Places the DHS Inspector General under the authority, direction, and control of the Secretary with respect to audits or investigations, or the issuance of subpoenas, that require access to sensitive information concerning intelligence, counterintelligence, or counterterrorism matters; criminal investigations or proceedings; undercover operations; the identify of confidential sources; and certain matters of disclosure.

Amends the Inspector General Act of 1978 to: (1) give such Inspector General oversight responsibility for internal investigations performed by the Office of Internal Affairs of the United States Customs Service and the Office of Inspections of the United States Secret Service; and (2) authorize each Inspector General, any Assistant Inspector General for Investigations, and any special agent supervised by such an Assistant Inspector General to carry a firearm, make arrests without warrants, and seek and execute warrants. Allows the latter only upon certain determinations by the Attorney General (exempts the Inspector General offices of various executive agencies from such requirement). Provides for the rescinding of such law enforcement powers. Requires the Inspector General offices exempted from the determinations requirement to collectively enter into a memorandum of understanding to establish an external review process for ensuring that adequate internal safeguards and management procedures continue to exist to ensure the proper utilization of such law enforcement powers within their departments.

Subtitle C: United States Secret Service – (Sec. 821) Transfers to the Secretary the functions of the United States Secret Service, which shall be maintained as a distinct entity within DHS.

Subtitle D: Acquisitions – (Sec. 831) Authorizes the Secretary to carry out a five-year pilot program under which the Secretary may exercise specified authorities in carrying out: (1) basic, applied, and advanced research and development projects for response to existing or emerging terrorist threats; and (2) defense prototype projects. Requires a report from the Comptroller General to specified congressional committees on the use of such authorities.

(Sec. 832) Permits the Secretary to procure temporary or intermittent: (1) services of experts or consultants; and (2) personal services without regard to certain pay limitations when necessary due to an urgent homeland security need.

(Sec. 833) Authorizes the Secretary to use specified micro purchase, simplified acquisition, and commercial item acquisition procedures with respect to any procurement made during the period beginning on the effective date of this Act and ending on September 30, 2007, if the Secretary determines that the mission of DHS would be seriously impaired without the use of such authorities. Requires a report from the Comptroller General.

(Sec. 834) Requires the Federal Acquisition Regulation to be revised to include regulations with regard to unsolicited proposals.

(Sec. 835) Prohibits the Secretary from entering into a contract with a foreign incorporated entity which is treated as an inverted domestic corporation. Sets forth requirements for such treatment. Authorizes the Secretary to waive such prohibition in the interest of homeland security, to prevent the loss of any jobs in the United States, or to prevent the Government from incurring any additional costs.

Subtitle E: Human Resources Management – (Sec. 841) Expresses the sense of Congress calling for the participation of DHS employees in the creation of the DHS human resources management system.

Amends Federal civil service law to authorize the Secretary, in regulations prescribed jointly with the Director of the Office of Personnel Management (OPM), to establish and adjust a human resources management system for organizational units of DHS. Requires the system to ensure that employees may organize, bargain collectively, and participate through labor organizations of their own choosing in decisions which affect them, subject to an exclusion from coverage or limitation on negotiability established by law. Imposes certain requirements upon the Secretary and the OPM Director to ensure the participation of employee representatives in the planning, development, and implementation of any human resources management system or system adjustments.

Declares the sense of Congress that DHS employees are entitled to fair treatment in any appeals that they bring in decisions relating to their employment.

Terminates all authority to issue regulations under this section five years after enactment of this Act.

(Sec. 842) Prohibits any agency or agency subdivision transferred to DHS from being excluded from coverage under labor-management relations requirements as a result of any order issued after June 18, 2002, unless: (1) the mission and responsibilities of the agency or subdivision materially change; and (2) a majority of the employees within the agency or subdivision have as their primary duty intelligence, counterintelligence, or investigative work directly related to terrorism investigation. Declares that collective bargaining units shall continue to be recognized unless such conditions develop. Prohibits exclusion of positions or employees for a bargaining unit unless the primary job duty materially changes or consists of intelligence, counterintelligence, or investigative work directly related to terrorism investigation. Waives these prohibitions and recognitions in circumstances where the President determines that their application would have a substantial adverse impact on the Department's ability to protect homeland security.

Subtitle F: Federal Emergency Procurement Flexibility – (Sec. 852) Provides that the simplified acquisition threshold to be applied for any executive agency procurement of property or services that is to be used to facilitate the defense against or recovery from terrorism or nuclear, biological, chemical, or radiological attack and that is carried out in support of a humanitarian or peacekeeping operation or a contingency operation shall be: (1) $200,000 for a contract to be awarded and performed, or a purchase to be made, inside the United States; or (2) $300,000 for a contract to be awarded and performed, or a purchase to be made, outside the United States.

(Sec. 854) Authorizes the head of each agency to designate certain employees to make such procurements below a micro-purchase threshold of $7,500 (currently $2,500) under the Office of Federal Procurement Policy Act.

(Sec. 855) Permits executive agencies to apply to any such procurement specified provisions of law relating to the procurement of commercial items, without regard to whether the property and services are commercial items. Makes the $5 million limitation on the use of simplified acquisition procedures inapplicable to purchases of property or services to which such provisions apply.

(Sec. 856) Requires executive agencies to use specified streamlined acquisition authorities and procedures for such procurements. Waives certain small business threshold requirements with respect to such procurements.

(Sec. 857) Requires the Comptroller General to review and report to specified congressional committees on the extent to which procurements of property and services have been made in accordance with requirements of this Subtitle.

(Sec. 858) Requires each executive agency to conduct market research to identify the capabilities of small businesses and new entrants into Federal contracting that are available to meet agency requirements in furtherance of defense against or recovery from terrorism or nuclear, biological, chemical, or radiological attack.

Subtitle G: Support Anti-terrorism by Fostering Effective Technologies Act of 2002 – Support Anti-terrorism by Fostering Effective Technologies Act of 2002 or SAFETY Act – (Sec. 862) Authorizes the Secretary to designate anti-terrorism technologies that qualify for protection under a risk management system in accordance with criteria that shall include: (1) prior Government use or demonstrated substantial utility and effectiveness; (2) availability for immediate deployment in public and private settings; (3) substantial likelihood that such technology will not be deployed unless protections under such system are extended; and (4) the magnitude of risk exposure to the public if such technology is not deployed. Makes the Secretary responsible for administration of such protections.

(Sec. 863) Provides a Federal cause of action for sellers suffering a loss from qualified anti-terrorism technologies so deployed. Prohibits punitive damages from being awarded against a seller.

(Sec. 864) Requires sellers of qualified anti-terrorism technologies to obtain liability insurance in amounts certified as satisfactory by the Secretary.

Subtitle H: Miscellaneous Provisions – (Sec. 871) Authorizes the Secretary to establish, appoint members of, and use the services of advisory committees as necessary.

(Sec. 872) Grants the Secretary limited authority to reorganize DHS by allocating or reallocating functions within it and by establishing, consolidating, altering, or discontinuing organizational units.

(Sec. 873) Requires the Secretary to comply with Federal requirements concerning the deposit of proceeds from property sold or transferred by the Secretary. Requires the President to submit to Congress a detailed Department budget request for FY 2004 and thereafter.

(Sec. 874) Requires each such budget request to be accompanied by a Future Years Homeland Security Program structured in the same manner as the annual Future Years Defense Program.

(Sec. 876) Provides that nothing in this Act shall confer upon the Secretary any authority to engage in war fighting, the military defense of the United States, or other military activities or limit the existing authority of the Department of Defense or the armed forces to do so.

(Sec. 878) Directs the Secretary to appoint a senior DHS official to assume primary responsibility for coordinating policy and operations within DHS and between DHS and other Federal departments and agencies with respect to interdicting the entry of illegal drugs into the United States and tracking and severing connections between illegal drug trafficking and terrorism.

(Sec. 879) Establishes within the Office of the Secretary an Office of International Affairs, headed by a Director, to: (1) promote information and education exchange on homeland security best practices and technologies with friendly nations; (2) identify areas for homeland security information and training exchange where the United States has a demonstrated weakness and another friendly nation has a demonstrated expertise; (3) plan and undertake international conferences, exchange programs, and training activities; and (4) manage international activities within DHS in coordination with other Federal officials with responsibility for counter-terrorism matters.

(Sec. 880) Prohibits any Government activity to implement the proposed component program of the Citizen Corps known as Operation TIPS (Terrorism Information and Prevention System).

(Sec. 881) Directs the Secretary to review the pay and benefit plans of each agency whose functions are transferred to DHS under this Act and to submit a plan for ensuring the elimination of disparities in pay and benefits throughout DHS, especially among law enforcement personnel, that are inconsistent with merit system principles.

(Sec. 882) Establishes within the Office of the Secretary the Office of National Capital Region Coordination, headed by a Director, to oversee and coordinate Federal homeland security programs for and relationships with State, local, and regional authorities within the National Capital Region. Requires an annual report from the Office to Congress on: (1) resources needed to fully implement homeland security efforts in the Region; (2) progress made by the Region in implementing such efforts; and (3) recommendations for additional needed resources to fully implement such efforts.

(Sec. 883) Requires DHS to comply with specified laws protecting equal employment opportunity and providing whistle blower protections.

(Sec. 885) Authorizes the Secretary to establish a permanent Joint Interagency Homeland Security Task Force, composed of representatives from military and civilian agencies, for the purpose of anticipating terrorist threats and taking actions to prevent harm to the United States.

(Sec. 886) Reaffirms the continued importance of Federal criminal code proscriptions on the use of the armed forces as posse comitatus and expresses the sense of Congress that nothing in this Act shall be construed to alter the applicability of such proscriptions to any use of the armed forces to execute the laws.

(Sec. 887) Requires the annual Federal response plan developed by DHS to be consistent with public health emergency provisions of the Public Health Service Act. Requires full disclosure of public health emergencies, or potential emergencies, among HHS, DHS, the Department of Justice, and the Federal Bureau of Investigation.

(Sec. 888) Transfers to DHS the authorities, functions, personnel, and assets of the Coast Guard, which shall be maintained as a distinct entity within DHS. Prohibits the Secretary from substantially or significantly reducing current Coast Guard missions or capabilities, with a waiver of such prohibition upon a declaration and certification to Congress that a clear, compelling and immediate need exists. Requires the DHS Inspector General to annually review and report to Congress on performance by the Coast Guard of its mission requirements. Requires the Commandant of the Coast Guard, upon its transfer, to report directly to the Secretary. Prohibits any of the above conditions and restrictions from applying to the Coast Guard when it is operating as a service in the Navy. Directs the Secretary to report to specified congressional committees on the feasibility of accelerating the rate of procurement in the Coast Guard's Integrated Deepwater System from 20 to ten years.

(Sec. 889) Requires the inclusion in the President's annual budget documents of a detailed homeland security funding analysis for the previous, current, and next fiscal years.

(Sec. 890) Amends the Air Transportation Safety and System Stabilization Act, with respect to the September 11th Victim Compensation Fund of 2001, to limit "agents" of an air carrier engaged in the business of providing air transportation security to persons that have contracted directly with the Federal Aviation Administration on or after February 17,

2002, to provide such security and that had not been or are not debarred within six months of that date.

Subtitle I: Information Sharing – Homeland Security Information Sharing Act – (Sec. 891) Expresses the sense of Congress that Federal, State, and local entities should share homeland security information to the maximum extent practicable, with special emphasis on hard-to-reach urban and rural communities.

(Sec. 892) Directs the President to prescribe and implement procedures for Federal agency: (1) sharing of appropriate homeland security information, including with DHS and appropriate State and local personnel; and (2) handling of classified information and sensitive but unclassified information. Authorizes appropriations.

(Sec. 893) Requires an implementation report from the President to the congressional intelligence and judiciary committees.

(Sec. 895) Amends the Federal Rules of Criminal Procedure to treat as contempt of court any knowing violation of guidelines jointly issued by the Attorney General and DCI with respect to disclosure of grand jury matters otherwise prohibited. Allows disclosure to appropriate Federal, State, local, or foreign government officials of grand jury matters involving a threat of grave hostile acts of a foreign power, domestic or international sabotage or terrorism, or clandestine intelligence gathering activities by an intelligence service or network of a foreign power (threat), within the United States or elsewhere. Permits disclosure to appropriate foreign government officials of grand jury matters that may disclose a violation of the law of such government. Requires State, local, and foreign officials to use disclosed information only in conformity with guidelines jointly issued by the Attorney General and the DCI.

(Sec. 896) Amends the Federal criminal code to authorize Federal investigative and law enforcement officers conducting communications interception activities, who have obtained knowledge of the contents of any intercepted communication or derivative evidence, to disclose such contents or evidence to: (1) a foreign investigative or law enforcement officer if the disclosure is appropriate to the performance of the official duties of the officer making or receiving the disclosure; and (2) any appropriate Federal, State, local, or foreign government official if the contents or evidence reveals such a threat, for the purpose of preventing or responding to such threat. Provides guidelines for the use and disclosure of the information.

(Sec. 897) Amends the Uniting and Strengthening America by Providing Appropriate Tools Required to Intercept and Obstruct Terrorism

Act (USA PATRIOT ACT) of 2001 to make lawful the disclosure to appropriate Federal, State, local, or foreign government officials of information obtained as part of a criminal investigation that reveals such a threat.

(Sec. 898) Amends the Foreign Intelligence Surveillance Act of 1978 to allow Federal officers who conduct electronic surveillance and physical searches in order to acquire foreign intelligence information to consult with State and local law enforcement personnel to coordinate efforts to investigate or protect against such a threat.

Title IX: National Homeland Security Council – (Sec. 901) Establishes within the Executive Office of the President the Homeland Security Council to advise the President on homeland security matters.

(Sec. 903) Includes as members of the Council: (1) the President; (2) the Vice President; (3) the Secretary; (4) the Attorney General; and (5) the Secretary of Defense.

(Sec. 904) Requires the Council to: (1) assess the objectives, commitments, and risks of the United States in the interest of homeland security and make recommendations to the President; and (2) oversee and review Federal homeland security policies and make policy recommendations to the President.

(Sec. 906) Authorizes the President to convene joint meetings of the Homeland Security Council and the National Security Council.

Title X: Information Security – Federal Information Security Management Act of 2002 – (Sec. 1001) Revises Government information security requirements. Requires the head of each agency operating or exercising control of a national security system to ensure that the agency: (1) provides information security protections commensurate with the risk and magnitude of the harm resulting from the unauthorized access, use, disclosure, disruption, modification, or destruction of the information; and (2) implements information security policies and practices as required by standards and guidelines for national security systems. Authorizes appropriations for FY 2003 through 2007.

(Sec. 1002) Transfers from the Secretary of Commerce to the Director of the Office of Management and Budget (OMB) the authority to promulgate information security standards pertaining to Federal information systems.

(Sec. 1003) Amends the National Institute of Standards and Technology Act to revise and expand the mandate of the National Institute of Standards and Technology to develop standards, guidelines, and associated methods and techniques for information systems. Renames the Computer System

Security and Privacy Advisory Board as the Information Security and Privacy Board and requires it to advise the Director of OMB (instead of the Secretary of Commerce) on information security and privacy issues pertaining to Federal Government information systems.

Title XI: Department of Justice Divisions – Subtitle A: Executive Office for Immigration Review – (Sec. 1101) Declares that there is in the Department of Justice (DOJ) the Executive Office for Immigration Review (EOIR), which shall be subject to the direction and regulation of the Attorney General under the INA.

(Sec. 1102) Amends the INA to grant the Attorney General such authorities and functions relating to the immigration and naturalization of aliens as were exercised by EOIR, or by the Attorney General with respect to EOIR, on the day before the effective date of the Immigration Reform, Accountability and Security Enhancement Act of 2002.

Subtitle B: Transfer of the Bureau of Alcohol, Tobacco and Firearms to the Department of Justice – (Sec. 1111) Establishes within DOJ, under the Attorney General's authority, the Bureau of Alcohol, Tobacco, Firearms, and Explosives (the Bureau). Transfers to DOJ the authorities, functions, personnel, and assets of the Bureau of Alcohol, Tobacco and Firearms (BATF), which shall be maintained as a distinct entity within DOJ, including the related functions of the Secretary of the Treasury.

Provides that the Bureau shall be headed by a Director and shall be responsible for: (1) investigating criminal and regulatory violations of the Federal firearms, explosives, arson, alcohol, and tobacco smuggling laws; (2) such transferred functions; and (3) any other function related to the investigation of violent crime or domestic terrorism that is delegated to the Bureau by the Attorney General.

Retains within the Department of the Treasury certain authorities, functions, personnel, and assets of BATF relating to the administration and enforcement of the Internal Revenue Code.

Establishes within the Department of the Treasury the Tax and Trade Bureau, which shall retain and administer the authorities, functions, personnel, and assets of BATF that are not transferred to DOJ.

(Sec. 1113) Amends the Federal criminal code to authorize special agents of the Bureau, as well as any other investigator or officer charged by the Attorney General with enforcing criminal, seizure, or forfeiture laws, to carry firearms, serve warrants and subpoenas, and make arrests without warrant for offenses committed in their presence or for felonies on reasonable grounds. Authorizes any special agent to make seizures of property subject to forfeiture to the United States. Sets forth provisions regarding seizure, disposition, and claims pertaining to property.

(Sec. 1114) Establishes within the Bureau an Explosives Training and Research Facility at Fort AP Hill in Fredericksburg, Virginia, to train Federal, State, and local law enforcement officers to: (1) investigate bombings and explosions; (2) properly handle, utilize, and dispose of explosive materials and devices; (3) train canines on explosive detection; and (4) conduct research on explosives. Authorizes appropriations.

(Sec. 1115) Transfers the Personnel Management Demonstration Project to the Attorney General for continued use by the Bureau and to the Secretary of the Treasury for continued use by the Tax and Trade Bureau.

Subtitle C: Explosives – Safe Explosives Act – (Sec. 1122) Rewrites Federal criminal code provisions regarding the purchase of explosives to create a new "limited permit" category. Prohibits a holder of a limited permit: (1) from transporting, shipping, causing to be transported, or receiving in interstate or foreign commerce explosive materials; (2) from receiving explosive materials from a licensee or permittee whose premises are located outside the holder's State of residence; or (3) on more than six separate occasions during the period of the permit, from receiving explosive materials from one or more licensees or permittees whose premises are located within the holder's State of residence.

Requires license, user permit, and limited permit applicants to include the names of and identifying information (including fingerprints and a photograph of each responsible person) regarding all employees who will be authorized by the applicant to possess explosive materials. Caps the fee for limited permits at $50 for each permit. Makes each limited permit valid for not longer than one year.

Modifies criteria for approving licenses and permits. Requires the Secretary of the Treasury to issue to the applicant the appropriate license or permit if, among other conditions: (1) the applicant is not a person who is otherwise prohibited from possessing explosive materials (excluded person); (2) the Secretary verifies by inspection or other appropriate means that the applicant has a place of storage for explosive materials that meets the Secretary's standards of public safety and security against theft (inapplicable to an applicant for renewal of a limited permit if the Secretary has verified such matters by inspection within the preceding three years); (3) none of the applicant's employees who will be authorized to possess explosive materials is an excluded person; and (4) in the case of a limited permit, the applicant has certified that the applicant will not

155

receive explosive materials on more than six separate occasions during the 12-month period for which the limited permit is valid. Authorizes the Secretary to inspect the storage places of an applicant for or holder of a limited permit only as provided under the code. Requires the Secretary of the Treasury to approve or deny an application for licenses and permits within 90 days.

Requires the Secretary: (1) upon receiving from an employer the name and other identifying information with respect to a person or an employee who will be authorized to possess explosive materials, to determine whether such person or employee is an excluded person; (2) upon determining that such person or employee is not an excluded person, to notify the employer and to issue to the person or employee a letter of clearance confirming the determination; and (3) upon determining that such person or employee is an excluded person, to notify the employer and issue to such person or employee a document that confirms the determination, explains the grounds, provides information on how the disability may be relieved, and explains how the determination may be appealed.

(Sec. 1123) Includes among aliens who may lawfully receive or possess explosive materials any alien who is in lawful non-immigrant status, is a refugee admitted under the INA, or is in asylum status under the INA and who is: (1) a foreign law enforcement officer of a friendly government; (2) a person having the power to direct the management and policies of a corporation; (3) a member of a North Atlantic Treaty Organization or other friendly foreign military force; or (4) lawfully present in the United States in cooperation with the DCI and the shipment, transportation, receipt, or possession of the explosive materials is in furtherance of such cooperation.

(Sec. 1124) Requires: (1) licensed manufacturers, licensed importers, and those who manufacture or import explosive materials or ammonium nitrate to furnish samples and relevant information when required by the Secretary; and (2) the Secretary to authorize reimbursement of the fair market value of samples furnished, as well as reasonable shipment costs.

(Sec. 1125) Sets penalties for the destruction of property of institutions receiving Federal financial assistance.

(Sec. 1127) Requires a holder of a license or permit to report any theft of explosive materials to the Secretary not later than 24 hours after discovery. Sets penalties for failure to report.

(Sec. 1128) Authorizes appropriations.

Title XII: Airline War Risk Insurance Legislation – (Sec. 1201) Amends Federal aviation law to extend the period during which the

Secretary of Transportation may certify an air carrier as a victim of terrorism (and thus subject to the $100 million limit on aggregate third-party claims) for acts of terrorism from September 22, 2001, through December 31, 2003.

(Sec. 1202) Directs the Secretary of Transportation to extend through August 31, 2003, and authorizes the Secretary to extend through December 31, 2003, the termination date of any insurance policy that the Department of Transportation (DOT) issues to an American aircraft or foreign-flag aircraft against loss or damage arising out of any risk from operation, and that is in effect on enactment of this Act, on no less favorable terms to such air carrier than existed on June 19, 2002. Directs the Secretary, however, to amend such policy to add coverage for losses or injuries to aircraft hulls, passengers, and crew at the limits carried by air carriers for such losses and injuries as of such enactment, and at an additional premium comparable to the premium charged for third-party casualty under the policy.

Limits the total premium paid by an air carrier for such a policy to twice the premium it was paying for its third party policy as of June 19, 2002. Declares that coverage in such a policy shall begin with the first dollar of any covered loss incurred.

(Sec. 1204) Directs the Secretary of Transportation to report to specified congressional committees concerning: (1) the availability and cost of commercial war risk insurance for air carriers and other aviation entities for passengers and third parties; (2) the economic effect upon such carriers and entities of available commercial war risk insurance; and (3) the manner in which DOT could provide an alternative means of providing aviation war risk reinsurance covering passengers, crew, and third parties through use of a risk-retention group or by other means.

Title XIII: Federal Workforce Improvement – Subtitle A: Chief Human Capital Officers – Chief Human Capital Officers Act of 2002 – (Sec. 1302) Requires the heads of Federal departments and agencies currently required to have a Chief Financial Officer to appoint or designate a Chief Human Capital Officer to: (1) advise and assist agency officials in selecting, developing, training, and managing a high-quality, productive workforce in accordance with merit system principles; and (2) implement the rules and regulations of the President and the Office of OPM and civil service laws.

Requires such Officer's functions to include: (1) setting the agency's workforce development strategy; (2) assessing workforce characteristics and future needs; (3) aligning the agency's human resources policies and

157

programs with organization mission, strategic goals, and performance outcomes; (4) developing and advocating a culture of continuous learning to attract and retain employees with superior abilities; (5) identifying best practices and benchmarking studies; and (6) applying methods for measuring intellectual capital and identifying links of that capital to organizational performance and growth.

(Sec. 1303) Establishes a Chief Human Capital Officers Council (consisting of the Director of OPM, the Deputy Director for Management of the Office of Management and Budget, and the Chief Human Capital Officers of executive departments and other members designated by the Director of OPM) to advise and coordinate the activities of the agencies of its members on such matters as modernization of human resources systems, improved quality of human resources information, and legislation affecting human resources operations and organizations.

(Sec. 1304) Directs OPM to design a set of systems, including metrics, for assessing the management of human capital by Federal agencies.

Subtitle B: Reforms Relating to Federal Human Capital Management – (Sec. 1311) Requires each agency's: (1) performance plan to describe how its performance goals and objectives are to be achieved; and (2) program performance report to include a review of the goals and evaluation of the plan relative to the agency's strategic human capital management.

(Sec. 1312) Authorizes the President to prescribe rules which grant authority for agencies to appoint candidates directly to certain positions for which there exists a severe candidate shortage or a critical hiring need.

Allows OPM to establish quality category rating systems for evaluating applicants for competitive service positions under two or more quality categories based on merit rather than numerical ratings. Requires agencies that establish a quality category rating system to report to Congress on that system, including information on the number of employees hired, the impact that system has had on the hiring of veterans and minorities, and the way in which managers were trained in the administration of it.

(Sec. 1313) Sets forth provisions governing Federal employee voluntary separation incentive payments. Requires each agency, before obligating any resources for such payments, to submit to OPM for modification and approval a plan outlining the intended use of such payments and a proposed organizational chart for the agency once such payments have been completed. Requires such plan to include the positions and functions affected, the categories of employees to be offered such payments, the timing and amounts of payments, and how the agency will subsequently operate. Limits voluntary separation incentive payments to the lesser of: (1) the amount of severance pay to which an employee would be entitled; or (2) an amount determined by the agency head, not to exceed $25,000. Sets forth provisions regarding the repayment and waiver of repayment of such incentive payments upon subsequent employment with the Government. Authorizes the Director of the Administrative Office of the United States Courts to establish a substantially similar program for the judicial branch. Continues existing voluntary separation incentives authority until expiration.

Amends Federal employee early retirement provisions to apply to employees who are: (1) voluntarily separated by an agency undergoing substantial delayering, reorganization, reductions in force, functions transfer, or workforce restructuring; or (2) identified as being in positions that are becoming surplus or excess to the agency's future ability to carry out its mission effectively; and (3) within the scope of the offer of voluntary early retirement on the basis of specific periods or such employee's organizational unit, occupational series, geographical location, and/or skills, knowledge, and other factors related to a position. Expresses the sense of Congress that the implementation of this section is intended to reshape, and not downsize, the Federal workforce.

(Sec. 1314) Includes students who provide voluntary services for the Government as "employees" for purposes of provisions authorizing agency programs to encourage employees to commute by means other than single-occupancy motor vehicles.

Subtitle C: Reforms Relating to the Senior Executive Service – (Sec. 1321) Repeals recertification requirements for senior executives.

(Sec. 1322) Changes the limitation on total annual compensation (basic pay and cash payments) from the annual rate of basic pay payable for level I of the Executive Schedule to the total annual compensation payable to the Vice President for certain senior level executive and judicial employees who hold a position in or under an agency that has been certified as having a performance appraisal system which makes meaningful distinctions based on relative performance.

Subtitle D: Academic Training – (Sec. 1331) Revises agency academic degree training criteria to allow agencies to select and assign employees to academic degree training and to pay and reimburse such training costs if such training: (1) contributes significantly to meeting an agency training need, resolving an agency staffing problem, or accomplishing goals in the agency's strategic plan; (2) is part of a planned, systemic, and coordinated agency employee development program linked to accomplishing such goals; and (3) is accredited and is provided by a college or university that is accredited by a nationally recognized body.

(Sec. 1332) Amends the David L. Boren National Security Education Act of 1991 to modify service agreement requirements for recipients of scholarships and fellowships under the National Security Education Program to provide for recipients to work in other Federal offices or agencies when no national security position is available.

Title XIV: Arming Pilots Against Terrorism – Arming Pilots Against Terrorism Act – (Sec. 1402) Amends Federal law to direct the Under Secretary of Transportation for Security (in the Transportation Security Administration) to establish a two-year pilot program to: (1) deputize volunteer pilots of air carriers as Federal law enforcement officers to defend the flight decks of aircraft against acts of criminal violence or air piracy (Federal flight deck officers); and (2) provide training, supervision, and equipment for such officers.

Requires the Under Secretary to begin the process of training and deputizing qualified pilots to be Federal flight deck officers under the program. Allows the Under Secretary to request another Federal agency to deputize such officers.

Directs the Under Secretary to authorize flight deck officers to carry firearms and to use force, including lethal force, according to standards and circumstances the Under Secretary prescribes. Shields air carriers from liability for damages in Federal or State court arising out of a Federal flight deck officer's use of or failure to use a firearm. Shields flight deck officers from liability for acts or omissions in defending the flight deck of an aircraft against acts of criminal violence or air piracy, except in cases of gross negligence or willful misconduct.

Declares that if an accidental discharge of a firearm results in the injury or death of a passenger or crew member on the aircraft, the Under Secretary: (1) shall revoke the deputization of the responsible Federal flight deck officer if such discharge was attributable to the officer's negligence; and (2) may temporarily suspend the pilot program if the Under Secretary determines that a shortcoming in standards, training, or procedures was responsible for the accidental discharge.

Prohibits an air carrier from prohibiting a pilot from becoming a Federal flight deck officer, or threatening any retaliatory action against the pilot for doing so.

Declares the sense of Congress that the Federal air marshal program is critical to aviation security, and that nothing in this Act shall be construed as preventing the Under Secretary from implementing and training Federal air marshals.

(Sec. 1403) Directs the Under Secretary, in updating the guidance for training flight and cabin crews, to issue a rule to: (1) require both classroom and effective hands-on situational training in specified elements of self-defense; (2) require training in the proper conduct of a cabin search, including the duty time required to conduct it; (3) establish the required number of hours of training and the qualifications for training instructors; (4) establish the intervals, number of hours, and elements of recurrent training; (5) ensure that air carriers provide the initial training within 24 months of the enactment of this Act. Directs the Under Secretary to designate an official in the Transportation Security Administration to be responsible for overseeing the implementation of the training program; and (6) ensure that no person is required to participate in any hands-on training activity that such person believes will have an adverse impact on his or her health or safety.

Amends the Aviation and Transportation Security Act to authorize the Under Secretary to take certain enhanced security measures, including to require that air carriers provide flight attendants with a discreet, hands-free, wireless method of communicating with the pilot of an aircraft.

Directs the Under Secretary to study and report to Congress on the benefits and risks of providing flight attendants with nonlethal weapons to aide in combating air piracy and criminal violence on commercial airlines.

(Sec. 1404) Directs the Secretary of Transportation to study and report within six months to Congress on: (1) the number of armed Federal law enforcement officers (other than Federal air marshals) who travel on commercial airliners annually, and the frequency of their travel; (2) the cost and resources necessary to provide such officers with supplemental aircraft anti-terrorism training comparable to the training that Federal air marshals receive; (3) the cost of establishing a program at a Federal law enforcement training center for the purpose of providing new Federal law enforcement recruits with standardized training comparable to Federal air marshal training; (4) the feasibility of implementing a certification program designed to ensure that Federal law enforcement officers have completed aircraft anti-terrorism training, and track their travel over a six-month period; and (5) the feasibility of staggering the flights of such officers to ensure the maximum amount of flights have a certified trained Federal officer on board.

(Sec. 1405) Amends Federal aviation law to require the Under Secretary to respond within 90 days of receiving a request from an air carrier for authorization to allow pilots of the air carrier to carry less-than-lethal weapons.

Title XV: Transition – Subtitle A: Reorganization Plan – (Sec. 1502) Requires the President, within 60 days after enactment of this Act, to transmit to the appropriate congressional committees a reorganization plan regarding: (1) the transfer of agencies, personnel, assets, and obligations to DHS pursuant to this Act; and (2) any consolidation, reorganization, or streamlining of agencies transferred to DHS pursuant to this Act.

(Sec. 1503) Expresses the sense of Congress that each House of Congress should review its committee structure in light of the reorganization of responsibilities within the executive branch by the establishment of DHS.

Subtitle B: Transitional Provisions – (Sec. 1511) Outlines transitional provisions with regard to assistance from officials having authority before the effective date of this Act; details of personnel and services to assist in the transition; acting officials during the transition period; the transfer of personnel, assets, obligations and functions; and the status of completed administrative actions, pending proceedings and civil actions, and Inspector General oversight. Prohibits DHS use of any funds derived from the Highway Trust Fund, the Airport and Airway Trust Fund, the Inland Waterway Trust Fund, or the Harbor Maintenance Trust Fund, with a specified exception for certain security-related funds provided to the Federal Aviation Administration.

(Sec. 1514) Provides that nothing in this Act shall be construed to authorize the development of a national identification system or card.

(Sec. 1516) Authorizes and directs the Director of OMB to make additional necessary incidental dispositions of personnel, assets, and liabilities in connection with the functions transferred by this Act.

Title XVI: Corrections to Existing Law Relating to Airline Transportation Security – (Sec. 1601) Amends Federal aviation law to require the Administrator of the Federal Aviation Administration (FAA), along with the Under Secretary of Transportation for Security, to each conduct research (including behavioral research) and development activities to develop, modify, test, and evaluate a system, procedure, facility, or device to protect passengers and property against acts of criminal violence, aircraft piracy, and terrorism and to ensure security.

Directs the Secretary of Transportation (currently, the Under Secretary) to prescribe regulations prohibiting disclosure of information obtained or developed in ensuring security under this section if the Secretary of Transportation decides disclosing such information would: (1) be an unwarranted invasion of personal privacy; (2) reveal a trade secret or privileged or confidential commercial or financial information; or (3) be detrimental to the safety of passengers in transportation. Sets forth similar provisions requiring the Under Secretary to prescribe regulations prohibiting the disclosure of information obtained or developed in carrying out security under authority of the Aviation and Transportation Security Act (PL107–71).

(Sec. 1602) Increases the maximum civil penalty to $25,000 for a person who violates certain aviation security requirements while operating an aircraft for the transportation of passengers or property for compensation (except an individual serving as an airman).

(Sec. 1603) Revises certain hiring security screener standards to allow a national (currently, only a citizen) of the United States to become a security screener.

Title XVII: Conforming and Technical Amendments – (Sec. 1701) Sets forth technical and conforming amendments.

(Sec. 1706) Transfers from the Administrator of General Services to the Secretary of Homeland Security law enforcement authority for the protection of Federal property.

(Sec. 1708) Establishes in DOD a National Bio-Weapons Defense Analysis Center to develop countermeasures to potential attacks by terrorists using weapons of mass destruction.

(Sec. 1714) Amends the Public Health Service Act to define "vaccine" to mean any preparation or suspension, including one containing an attenuated or inactive microorganism or toxin, developed or administered to produce or enhance the body's immune response to a disease and to include all components and ingredients listed in the vaccine's product license application and product label.

APPENDIX E
Intelligence Reform and Terrorism Act of 2004

Intelligence Reform and Terrorism Prevention Act of 2004 – **Title I: Reform of the Intelligence Community** – National Security Intelligence Reform Act of 2004 – **Subtitle A: Establishment of Director of National Intelligence** – (Sec. 1011) Amends the National Security Act of 1947 to establish a Director of National Intelligence (Director), to be appointed by the President with the advice and consent of the Senate. Requires the Director to have extensive national security expertise. Prohibits the Director from being located within the Executive Office of the President or simultaneously serving as head of the Central Intelligence Agency (CIA) or any other intelligence community (IC) element.

Gives the Director primary responsibility for: (1) serving as head of the IC; (2) acting as principal adviser for intelligence matters related to national security; and (3) managing, overseeing, and directing the execution of the National Intelligence Program (formerly known as the National Foreign Intelligence Program). Requires the Director to ensure that timely, objective, and independent national intelligence based upon all available sources is provided to: (1) the President; (2) the heads of departments and agencies of the executive branch; (3) the Chairman of the Joint Chiefs of Staff and senior military commanders; and (4) the Senate and House of Representatives and congressional committees.

Gives the Director access to all national intelligence and intelligence related to national security collected by Federal entities, unless otherwise directed by the President.

Outlines budgetary duties of the Director, including: (1) the development of an annual consolidated budget for the National Intelligence Program (the Program); and (2) participation in the development of annual budgets for the Joint Military Intelligence Program and for Tactical Intelligence and Related Activities.

Requires the Director to manage funds appropriated for the Program.

Authorizes the Director to: (1) transfer and reprogram funds within the Program, with the approval of the Director of the Office of Management and Budget (OMB) and after consultation with the affected agencies; and (2) transfer IC element personnel to the national intelligence center or to other IC elements, with the OMB Director's approval and after notice to specified congressional committees.

Requires the Director to, among other things: (1) develop standards for the collection and dissemination of national intelligence; (2) oversee the National Counterterrorism Center (NCC) established by this Act; (3) prescribe personnel policies for the IC; (4) ensure compliance with the law by the CIA and other IC elements; (5) promote intelligence information sharing within the IC; (6) make intelligence analysis a priority within the IC; (7) implement guidelines for the protection of intelligence sources and methods; (8) oversee the coordination of the relationships between IC elements and their foreign counterparts; (9) establish requirements and priorities for the collection of foreign intelligence information under the Foreign Intelligence Surveillance Act of 1978 (FISA) and assist the Attorney General in the dissemination of information collected under FISA-related searches and surveillance; and (10) develop an enterprise architecture for the IC.

Requires the Director: (1) subject to the direction of the President, to establish uniform procedures for access to sensitive compartmented information; (2) subject to the direction of the President and after consultation with the Secretary of Defense, to ensure that Program budgets for IC elements within the Department of Defense (DOD) are adequate; and (3) to coordinate performance by IC elements within the Program in areas of common concern.

Establishes an Office of the Director of National Intelligence and related positions.

Establishes a National Intelligence Council to produce national intelligence estimates for the U.S. Government and evaluate the collection and production of intelligence by the IC.

Establishes within the Office of the Director, among other positions: (1) a Civil Liberties Protection Officer; (2) a Director of Science and Technology; and (3) a National Counterintelligence Executive.

Specifies the functions of the CIA and the CIA Director.

(Sec. 1012) Amends the National Security Act of 1947 to redefine "national intelligence" and "intelligence related to national security" to refer to all intelligence, regardless of the source, that pertains to more than one Government agency and involves: (1) threats to the United States, its people, property, or interests; (2) the development, proliferation, or use of weapons of mass destruction (WMDs); or (3) any other matter bearing on national or homeland security.

(Sec. 1013) Requires the Director, in consultation with the Secretary of Defense and the Director of the CIA, to develop joint procedures to be used by the DOD and the CIA to improve operational coordination.

(Sec. 1014) Gives the Director a role in the appointment of certain intelligence officials.

(Sec. 1016) Requires the President to establish a secure information sharing environment (ISE) for the sharing of intelligence and related information in a manner consistent with national security and the protection of privacy and civil liberties, incorporating specified attributes.

Establishes an Information Sharing Council to assist the President and the ISE program manager with ISE-related duties.

(Sec. 1017) Requires the Director to establish a process and assign responsibility for ensuring that elements of the IC conduct alternative ("-red-team") analysis of information and conclusions in IC products.

(Sec. 1018) Directs the President to issue guidelines ensuring the effective implementation of the Director's authorities in a manner that does not abrogate the statutory responsibilities of Federal agency heads.

(Sec. 1019) Requires the Director to assign responsibility for ensuring the timeliness and analytical integrity of IC products.

Requires the preparation of reports relating to the requirements of this subtitle.

Subtitle B: National Counterterrorism Center, National Counter Proliferation Center, and National Intelligence Centers – (Sec. 1021) Establishes the National Counterterrorism Center (NCC) to: (1) analyze and integrate all U.S. intelligence pertaining to terrorism and counterterrorism; (2) conduct strategic operational planning for counterterrorism activities; (3) ensure that intelligence agencies have access to, and receive, all intelligence needed to accomplish their missions; and (4) serve as the central and shared knowledge bank on known and suspected terrorists and international terror groups.

Authorizes the Center to receive intelligence pertaining exclusively to domestic counterterrorism.

Sets forth the duties and responsibilities of the Center's Director including, among other things: (1) serving as the principal advisor to the Director on intelligence operations relating to counterterrorism; and (2) taking primary responsibility within the U.S. Government for conducting net assessments of terrorist threats.

Requires the NCC Director to establish within the NCC a Directorate of Strategic Operational Planning.

(Sec. 1022) Amends the National Security Act of 1947 to require the President to establish a National Counter Proliferation Center.

(Sec. 1023) Authorizes the Director to establish National Intelligence Centers to address intelligence priorities, including but not limited to regional issues.

Subtitle C: Joint Intelligence Community Council – (Sec. 1031) Establishes a Joint Intelligence Community Council (JICC) to assist the Director in developing and implementing a joint, unified national intelligence effort to protect national security. Authorizes any member of the JICC to make recommendations to Congress.

Subtitle D: Improvement of Education for the Intelligence Community – (Sec. 1041) Requires the Director to identify the linguistic requirements for the Office of the Director of National Intelligence, identify the specific requirements for the range of linguistic skills necessary for the IC, and develop a comprehensive plan for the Office to meet such requirements through the education, recruitment, and training of linguists.

Requires the Director to require heads of each element and component within the Office with responsibility for professional intelligence training to periodically review and revise the curriculum for such training for senior and intermediate level personnel.

(Sec. 1042) Requires the Director to provide for the cross-disciplinary education and training of IC personnel.

(Sec. 1043) Requires the Director to establish an Intelligence Community Scholarship Program with a post-scholarship period of obligated civilian service of 24 months for each academic year of the scholarship.

Subtitle E: Additional Improvements of Intelligence Activities – (Sec. 1051) States that the Director, in cooperation with the Secretaries of Defense and Energy, should seek to ensure that each DOD service laboratory and each Department of Energy national laboratory may assist the Director in all aspects of technical intelligence and make their resources available to the IC.

(Sec. 1052) Expresses the sense of Congress that: (1) the Director should establish an intelligence center to coordinate the collection, analysis, production, and dissemination of open source intelligence to IC elements; (2) open source intelligence is valuable and must be integrated into the intelligence cycle; and (3) the intelligence center should ensure that each IC element uses open source intelligence consistent with its mission.

Requires the Director to report on the Director's decision regarding the establishment of an intelligence center.

(Sec. 1053) Authorizes the Director to provide for the establishment and training of a National Intelligence Reserve Corps for the temporary employment on a voluntary basis of former IC employees during periods of emergency.

Subtitle F: Privacy and Civil Liberties – (Sec. 1061) Establishes within the Executive Office of the President a Privacy and Civil Liberties Oversight Board to: (1) analyze and review actions taken by the Executive branch to protect the Nation from terrorism, ensuring a balance with privacy and civil liberties protections; and (2) ensure that liberty concerns are appropriately considered in the development and implementation of laws, regulations, and policies related to efforts to protect the Nation against terrorism. Requires annual reports on major Board activities.

Subtitle G: Conforming and Other Amendments – (Sec. 1071) Makes conforming amendments to existing law relating to the Director's role, the role of the CIA Director, and other matters.

(Sec. 1074) Redesignates the National Foreign Intelligence Program as the National Intelligence Program.

(Sec. 1078) Amends the Inspector General Act of 1978 to authorize the Director to establish an Office of Inspector General.

Subtitle H: Transfer, Termination, Transition and Other Provisions – (Sec. 1091) Transfers: (1) such staff of the Community Management Staff to the Office of the National Intelligence Director as the Director deems appropriate; and (2) the Terrorist Threat Integration Center to the NCC.

(Sec. 1093) Terminates the positions of Assistant Director of Central Intelligence for Collection, Assistant Director of Central Intelligence for Analysis and Production, and Assistant Director of Central Intelligence for Administration.

(Sec. 1094) Requires the President to transmit to Congress a plan for implementation of this title.

(Sec. 1095) Requires the Director to submit a report on progress made in implementing this title.

Subtitle I: Other Matters – (Sec. 1101) Requires the Secretary of Defense to study and report to specified congressional committees on promotion selection rates, and selection rates for professional military school attendance, of intelligence officers of the Armed Forces in comparison to the rates for other officers of the Armed Forces.

(Sec. 1102) Amends the Public Interest Declassification Act of 2000 to require the Public Interest Declassification Board to report directly to the President or, upon the President's designation, to the Vice President, Attorney General, or other designee (but precludes designation to an agency head or official who is authorized to classify information).

Adds to the list of purposes of the Board reviewing and making recommendations to the President with respect to any congressional requests to declassify or reconsider declassification of records.

Requires the Board to conduct declassification reviews upon the President's request.

Title II: Federal Bureau of Investigation – (Sec. 2001) Directs the Director of the Federal Bureau of Investigation (hereinafter FBI Director) to continue efforts to improve the intelligence capabilities of the FBI and to develop and maintain within the FBI a national intelligence workforce.

Requires the FBI Director to: (1) develop and maintain a specialized and integrated national intelligence workforce of agents, analysts, linguists, and surveillance specialists who are recruited, trained, and rewarded in a manner that creates an institutional culture in the FBI with substantial expertise in, and commitment to, the intelligence mission of the FBI; (2) establish career positions in national intelligence matters: (3) recruit agents with backgrounds and skills relevant to the intelligence mission of the FBI; (4) provide agents with training in intelligence and opportunities for assignments in national intelligence matters; and (5) make advanced training and work in intelligence matters a precondition to employee advancement.

Requires each direct supervisor of a Field Intelligence Group, and each Bureau Operation Manager at the Section Chief and Assistant Special Agent in Charge level and above to be a certified intelligence officer.

Requires the FBI Director to: (1) ensure that each Field Intelligence Group reports directly to a field office senior manager responsible for intelligence matters; (2) provide for necessary expansion of secure facilities in FBI field offices to meet the intelligence mission of the FBI; and (3) ensure the integration of analysts, agents, linguists, and surveillance personnel in the field.

Requires the FBI Director to establish a budget structure that reflects the four principal missions of the Bureau (i.e., intelligence, counterterrorism and counterintelligence, criminal enterprises/Federal crimes, and criminal justice services).

Requires the FBI Director to submit periodic reports to Congress on progress in carrying out improvements in FBI intelligence capabilities, including reports on FBI priorities, personnel reviews, and implementation of information-sharing principles.

(Sec. 2002) Redesignates the Office of Intelligence as the Directorate of Intelligence of the Federal Bureau of Investigation (Directorate). Assigns to the Directorate responsibility for intelligence functions, including: (1) supervision of all FBI national intelligence programs; (2) oversight of FBI field intelligence operations; (3) strategic analysis; (4) budget management; and (5) other responsibilities specified by the FBI Director or by law.

(Sec. 2003) Authorizes the FBI Director to establish career positions for intelligence analysts within the FBI; (2) establish an FBI Reserve Service (limited to 500 employees) for the temporary reemployment (no more than 180 days) of former FBI employees during periods of emergency; and (3) through FY 2007, for up to 50 employees per fiscal year, extend the mandatory retirement age for FBI employees to 65 (current law allows an extension to age 60).

(Sec. 2006) Requires the Attorney General to report annually to the House and Senate Committees on the Judiciary on FBI use of translators.

Title III: Security Clearances – (Sec. 3001) Directs the President to select a single executive branch department, agency, or element (designated entity) to be responsible for security clearances and investigations.

Requires all Federal agencies to accept security clearance background investigations and determinations that are completed by an authorized investigative agency or authorized adjudicative agency.

Directs the Director of the Office of Personnel Management (OPM) to establish and operate an integrated, secure database on security clearances.

Requires the head of the designated entity to evaluate the use of available information technology and databases in security clearance investigations and adjudications.

Requires: (1) the head of the designated entity to develop a plan to reduce the length of the personnel security clearance process; (2) such plan to provide for determinations on at least 90 percent of all security clearance applications within 60 days; and (3) implementation of such plan within five years after enactment of this Act.

Requires the head of the designated entity to report to Congress annually through 2011 on progress in meeting the requirements of this Act.

Authorizes appropriations.

Title IV: Transportation Security – Subtitle A: National Strategy for Transportation Security – (Sec. 4001) Requires the Secretary of

Homeland Security to: (1) develop and implement a National Strategy for Transportation Security and transportation modal security plans; and (2) submit such plans and periodic progress reports to appropriate congressional committees.

States that the strategy shall be the governing document for Federal transportation security efforts.

Subtitle B: Aviation Security – (Sec. 4011) Requires the issuance of guidance for the use of biometric or other technology that positively verifies the identity of each employee and law enforcement officer who enters a secure area of an airport.

Requires the Assistant Secretary of Homeland Security (Transportation Security Administration (TSA)) (hereinafter Assistant Secretary) to establish a uniform travel credential for Federal, State, and local law enforcement officers that incorporates biometrics and a process for using such credential to verify officer identity for purposes of carrying weapons on board aircraft.

Authorizes appropriations for: (1) research and development of advanced biometric technology applications to aviation security, including mass identification technology; and (2) the establishment of a competitive center of excellence to develop and expedite the Federal Government's use of biometric identifiers.

(Sec. 4012) Requires the Assistant Secretary to begin testing an advanced airline passenger prescreening system no later than January 1, 2005, that will allow the Department of Homeland Security (DHS) to compare passenger information with automatic selectee and no-fly lists.

Requires the Assistant Secretary to establish a process by which operators of charter aircraft or rental aircraft with a maximum take-off weight of more than 12,500 pounds may request DHS to use the advanced passenger prescreening system to compare information about individuals seeking to charter or rent such aircraft and any proposed passengers with automatic selectee and no-fly lists. Directs the Assistant Secretary to establish a timely and fair process for individuals identified as a threat to appeal that determination and correct erroneous information.

Directs the Secretary to issue notice of a proposed rulemaking that will allow DHS to compare passenger names for inbound or outbound international flights against the consolidated and integrated terrorist watchlist maintained by the Federal Government (terrorist watchlist). Requires the creation of a related appeal process.

Requires preparation of reports on: (1) the impact of automatic selectee and no-fly lists on privacy and civil liberties; and (2) the Terrorist Screening Center consolidated watchlist, including criteria for placing names on that list.

(Sec. 4013) Requires the Assistant Secretary to: (1) give high priority to airport screening checkpoint technology that will detect nonmetallic weapons and explosives; (2) transmit to the appropriate congressional committees a strategic plan to promote optimal use and deployment of explosive detection devices at airports; (3) take appropriate interim action until measures are implemented that enable the screening of all passengers for explosives; (4) develop a pilot program to deploy and test advanced airport checkpoint screening devices and technologies at not less than five U.S. airports; and (5) take necessary action to improve the job performance of airport screening personnel.

(Sec. 4016) Requires the Director of the Federal Air Marshal Service to continue developing operational initiatives to protect Federal air marshal anonymity.

Requires the Assistant Secretary for Immigration and Customs Enforcement (ICE) and the Director of the Federal Air Marshal Service to: (1) provide training on in-flight counterterrorism and weapons handling procedures and tactics to Federal law enforcement officers who fly while in possession of a firearm; and (2) ensure that TSA screeners and Federal Air Marshals, as well as Federal and local law enforcement agencies in States that border Canada or Mexico, receive training in identifying fraudulent identification documents, including fraudulent or expired visas or passports.

(Sec. 4017) Encourages the President to aggressively pursue international agreements with foreign governments to allow the maximum deployment of Federal air marshals on international flights.

(Sec. 4018) Authorizes the Assistant Secretary for ICE, after consultation with the Secretary of State, to direct the Federal Air Marshal Service to provide training to foreign law enforcement personnel.

(Sec. 4019) Directs the Assistant Secretary to: (1) take necessary action to expedite installation and use of advanced in-line baggage screening equipment at airports where screening is required; and (2) submit to appropriate congressional committees' schedules for expediting installation of such equipment and for replacing trace-detection equipment.

Requires the President to submit a cost-sharing study regarding installation of in-line baggage screening equipment.

Authorizes increased appropriations through FY 2007 for expiring and new letters of intent regarding airport security improvement projects.

(Sec. 4020) Requires the Under Secretary for Border and Transportation Security of DHS to provide assistance for acquisition and installation of security monitoring cameras in checked baggage screening areas not open to public view in those airports that are required to perform screening.

(Sec. 4021) Directs the Assistant Secretary, in consultation with the Administrator of the Federal Aviation Administration (FAA), to study the viability of providing devices or methods to enable flight crews to discreetly notify pilots in the case of security breaches or safety issues in the cabin and to report results of the study.

(Sec. 4022) Requires the FAA Administrator to develop a system for issuing pilot's licenses with enhanced security features.

(Sec. 4023) Directs the Assistant Secretary to develop and submit to appropriate congressional committees standards for determining appropriate aviation security staffing for all airports at which screening is required.

Requires the Comptroller General to thereafter conduct an expedited analysis of, and submit a report on, such standards.

Directs the Secretary to study the feasibility of combining under the aegis of DHS the operations of Federal employees involved in commercial airport screening and aviation security-related functions.

(Sec. 4024) Requires the Secretary to establish a plan and guidelines for implementing improved explosive detection system equipment.

Authorizes appropriations for research and development of improved explosive detection systems for aviation security.

(Sec. 4025) Requires the Assistant Secretary to complete a review of the Prohibited Items List under current regulations within 60 days of enactment of this Act, revise that list to prohibit air passengers from carrying butane lighters, and make other appropriate modifications.

(Sec. 4026) Directs the President to pursue, on an urgent basis, strong diplomatic and cooperative efforts to limit the availability, transfer, and proliferation of MANPADS (shoulder-fired missiles) worldwide and report to Congress on such efforts.

(Sec. 4028) Requires the Assistant Secretary to report on the costs and benefits of using secondary flight deck barriers and whether such barriers should be mandated for all air carriers.

(Sec. 4029) Extends through FY 2006 the authorization of appropriations for aviation security.

Subtitle C: Air Cargo Security – (Sec. 4051) Requires the Assistant Secretary to carry out a pilot program to evaluate the use of blast-resistant containers for cargo and baggage on passenger aircraft.

(Sec. 4052) Directs the Assistant Secretary to develop technology to better identify, track, and screen air cargo.

Authorizes appropriations through FY 2007 for: (1) improving aviation security related to the transportation of cargo; and (2) research and development related to enhanced air cargo security technology and the deployment and installation of such technology.

Requires the Secretary to establish a competitive grant program to encourage the development of advanced air cargo security technology.

(Sec. 4053) Requires the Assistant Secretary, within 240 days of enactment of this Act, to issue a final rule in Docket Number TSA-2004–19515 to amend transportation security regulations to enhance and improve the security of air cargo.

(Sec. 4054) Requires the Secretary, in coordination with the Secretary of Defense and the FAA Administrator, to submit a report on international air cargo threats.

Subtitle D: Maritime Security – (Sec. 4071) Directs the Secretary to: (1) implement a procedure under which DHS compares information about cruise ship passengers and crew with a terrorist watchlist; (2) use information obtained by this comparison to prevent identified persons from boarding or to subject them to additional security scrutiny through the use of no transport and automatic selectee lists; (3) require, by rulemaking, that cruise ship operators provide passenger and crew information for purposes of such comparison; and (4) establish operating procedures and data integrity measures for no transport and automatic selectee lists.

(Sec. 4072) Establishes a deadlines for DHS to carry out security planning activities called for in the Maritime Transportation Security Act of 2002, including: (1) preparation of a national maritime transportation security plan; and (2) facility and vessel vulnerability assessments. Requires the Secretary of the department in which the Coast Guard is operating to submit to specified congressional committees a comprehensive program management plan for the transportation security card program required by that Act and other specified reports.

Subtitle E: General Provisions – (Sec. 4081) Sets forth definitions and the effective date of this title.

Title V: Border Protection, Immigration, and Visa Matters – Subtitle A: Advanced Technology Northern Border Security Pilot Program – (Sec.

5101) Authorizes the Secretary to carry out a pilot program to test advanced technologies to improve border security between ports of entry (POEs) along the northern border of the United States. Specifies the required features of such program. Requires coordination of such program among United States, State and local, and Canadian law enforcement and border security agencies.

(Sec. 5104) Requires the Secretary to report on the pilot program.

Subtitle B: Border and Immigration Enforcement – (Sec. 5201) Requires the Secretary to submit to the President and appropriate congressional committees a comprehensive plan for the systematic surveillance of the southwest border of the United States by remotely piloted aircraft.

(Sec. 5202) Requires the Secretary to increase: (1) the number of full-time Border Patrol agents by not less than 2,000 per fiscal year from FY 2006 through 2010; and (2) the number of full-time immigration and customs enforcement investigators by not less than 800 per fiscal year for the same period.

(Sec. 5204) Directs the Secretary to increase by not less than 8,000 in each of FY 2006 through 2010 the number of beds available for immigration detention and removal operations of DHS. Requires the Secretary to give priority for the use of these additional beds to the detention of individuals charged with removability or inadmissibility on security and related grounds.

Subtitle C: Visa Requirements – (Sec. 5301) Amends the Immigration and Nationality Act to require aliens age 14 through 79 who are applying for nonimmigrant visas to submit to in-person interviews with consular officers unless such interview is waived in specified circumstances.

Mandates in-person interviews for all aliens who: (1) are not nationals of the country in which they are applying for a visa; (2) were previously refused a visa; (3) are listed in the Consular Lookout and Support System; (4) are nationals of countries officially designated as state sponsors of terrorism; (5) are prohibited from obtaining a visa until a security advisory opinion or other Department of State clearance is issued; or (6) are identified as members of a high-risk group identified by the Secretary of State.

(Sec. 5304) Precludes judicial review of visa revocations or revocations of other travel documents by consular officers or the Secretary of State. Adds to the list of deportable aliens those nonimmigrants whose visas or other documentation authorizing admission were revoked (making such aliens immediately deportable).

Subtitle D: Immigration Reform – (Sec. 5401) Provides enhanced criminal penalties for unlawfully bringing in and harboring aliens in cases where: (1) the offense is part of an ongoing commercial organization or enterprise; (2) aliens were transported in groups of ten or more; (3) aliens were transported in a manner that endangered their lives; or (4) the aliens presented a life-threatening health risk to the people of the United States.

Requires the Secretary to implement an outreach program to educate the public in the United States and abroad about the penalties for unlawfully bringing in and harboring aliens.

(Sec. 5402) Renders deportable any alien who has received military-type training from or on behalf of a terrorist organization.

(Sec. 5403) Requires the Comptroller General to study and report on the extent to which weaknesses in the asylum system and the withholding of removal system have been or could be exploited by aliens with terrorist ties. Gives the Comptroller General access, for purposes of such study, to the applications and administrative and judicial records of alien applicants for asylum and withholding of removal.

Subtitle E: Treatment of Aliens Who Commit Acts of Torture, Extrajudicial Killings, or Other Atrocities Abroad – (Sec. 5501) Renders inadmissible and deportable those aliens who: (1) order, incite, assist, or otherwise participate in conduct outside the United States that would, if committed in the United States or by a U.S. national, be genocide; and (2) commit, order, incite, assist, or participate in acts of torture or extrajudicial killing as defined by U.S. law. Makes these amendments applicable to offenses committed before, on, or after the enactment of this Act.

(Sec. 5502) Designates as inadmissible and deportable foreign government officials who have at any time committed particularly severe violations of religious freedom.

(Sec. 5503) Provides for a waiver of inadmissibility premised on torture or extrajudicial killing for aliens seeking temporary admission as nonimmigrants, in the Attorney General's discretion. Precludes waivers for such aliens who have engaged in Nazi persecution or genocide.

(Sec. 5504) Bars a finding of good moral character (necessary for naturalization) for aliens who: (1) participated in Nazi persecution, genocide, torture, or extrajudicial killing; or (2) were responsible for particularly severe violations of religious freedom while serving as foreign government officials.

(Sec. 5505) Directs the Attorney General to: (1) establish within the Criminal Division of the Department of Justice an Office of Special Investigations to investigate and, where appropriate, take action to denaturalize any alien who participated in Nazi persecution, genocide, torture, or extrajudicial killing; (2) consult the Secretary in making determinations concerning the criminal prosecution or extradition of such aliens.

(Sec. 5506) Requires the Attorney General to submit a report on implementation of this subtitle.

Title VI: Terrorism Prevention – Subtitle A: Individual Terrorists as Agents of Foreign Powers – (Sec. 6001) Amends the Foreign Intelligence Surveillance Act of 1978 (FISA) to redefine "agent of a foreign power" to include any person who engages in international terrorism or activities in preparation for such terrorism (currently, limited to persons connected to foreign powers). Makes this amendment subject to a sunset provision in the USA PATRIOT Act of 2001 which generally provides for a sunset date of December 31, 2005.

(Sec. 6002) Requires the Attorney General to submit semiannual reports on the targets of FISA orders and related outcomes, including but not limited to the aggregate number of persons targeted for electronic surveillance, physical searches, pen registers, and records access.

Subtitle B: Money Laundering and Terrorist Financing – (Sec. 6101) Authorizes appropriations for technological improvements in mission-critical systems of the Financial Crimes Enforcement Network (FinCEN).

(Sec. 6102) Reauthorizes appropriations for the national money laundering and related financial crimes strategy, the financial crime-free communities support program, and grants to fight money laundering and related financial crimes.

Subtitle C: Money Laundering Abatement and Financial Antiterrorism Technical Corrections – International Money Laundering Abatement and Financial Antiterrorism Technical Corrections Act of 2004 – (Sec. 6202) Makes technical corrections to the International Money Laundering Abatement and Anti-Terrorist Financing Act of 2001.

(Sec. 6204) Amends that Act to delete congressional authority to review and terminate its provisions by joint resolution.

(Sec. 6205) Makes this subchapter retroactively effective as if included in the USA PATRIOT Act of 2001.

Subtitle D: Additional Enforcement Tools – (Sec. 6301) Authorizes the Treasury to produce currency, postage stamps, and other security documents for foreign governments subject to certain conditions.

(Sec. 6302) Directs the Secretary of the Treasury, following the submission of a related report, to prescribe regulations requiring selected financial institutions to report to FinCEN certain cross-border electronic transmittals of funds.

(Sec. 6303) Directs the President, acting through the Secretary of the Treasury, to submit to Congress a report evaluating the current status of U.S. efforts to curtail international financing of terrorism.

Amends the Federal Deposit Insurance Act and the Federal Credit Union Act to impose administrative and civil penalties on any person who: (1) has served as senior Federal bank examiner of a particular financial institution or insured credit union for two or more months during the final 12 months of Federal employment; and (2) knowingly accepts compensation as an employee, officer, director, or consultant from that institution (including its holding company, a subsidiary, or an affiliate) or credit union within one year after departure from Federal service. Authorizes waivers of this restriction where the relevant authority certifies that granting the waiver would not affect the integrity of the Government's supervisory program.

Subtitle E: Criminal History Background Checks – (Sec. 6401) Amends the PROTECT Act to extend to 30 months the length of the State Pilot Program and the Child Safety Pilot Program.

(Sec. 6402) Private Security Officer Employment Authorization Act of 2004 – Allows employers of private security officers who are authorized by regulation to request criminal history record information searches of such security officers through a State identification bureau (authorized employers) to submit fingerprints or other means of positive identification for purposes of such searches. Requires written consent from employees prior to such searches and employee access to any information received.

Establishes criminal penalties for the knowing and intentional use of information obtained through criminal history record information searches for purposes other than determining an individual's suitability for employment as a private security officer.

(Sec. 6403) Requires the Attorney General to report on all statutory requirements for criminal history checks by the Department of Justice or its components, including recommendations for improving, standardizing, and consolidating existing procedures.

Subtitle F: Grand Jury Information Sharing – (Sec. 6501) Amends the Federal Rules of Criminal Procedure to authorize disclosure of certain grand jury matters, including matters involving threats of terrorism, to foreign government officials.

Subtitle G: Providing Material Support to Terrorism – Material Support to Terrorism Prohibition Enhancement Act of 2004 – (Sec. 6602) Amends the Federal criminal code to establish criminal penalties for knowingly receiving military-type training from an organization designated as a foreign terrorist organization by the Secretary of State.

Provides extraterritorial Federal jurisdiction.

(Sec. 6603) Modifies the statute prohibiting the knowing provision of material support to terrorists or terrorist organizations. Clarifies the definition of several types of material support.

Provides extraterritorial Federal jurisdiction.

States that nothing in this section shall be construed or applied so as to abridge the exercise of First Amendment rights.

Prohibits the prosecution of any person for providing material support if such support was approved by the Secretary of State with the concurrence of the Attorney General.

Provides for the sunset of specified provisions contained in this section on December 31, 2006.

(Sec. 6604) Modifies the statute prohibiting terrorist financing to make punishable: (1) the concealment of the proceeds of funds can be prosecuted (in addition to concealment of the funds themselves); and (2) the concealment of funds when they are presently being used to support terrorism (in addition to past use).

Subtitle H: Stop Terrorist and Military Hoaxes Act of 2004 – Stop Terrorist and Military Hoaxes Act of 2004 – (Sec. 6702) Amends the Federal criminal code to provide criminal and civil penalties for false information concerning terrorist activities and military hoaxes.

(Sec. 6703) Increases statutory penalties for false statements to Federal authorities and for obstructing administrative or congressional proceedings if the matter relates to international or domestic terrorism. Requires the U.S. Sentencing Commission to amend the U.S. Sentencing Guidelines to increase the offense level for such offenses.

Subtitle I: Weapons of Mass Destruction Prohibition Improvement Act of 2004 – Weapons of Mass Destruction Prohibition Improvement Act of 2004 – (Sec. 6802) Expands the jurisdictional bases and scope of the prohibition against weapons of mass destruction (WMDs). Expands the definition of "restricted persons" subject to the prohibition on possession or transfer of biological agents or toxins to include individuals acting for a country determined to have provided repeated support for international terrorism. Includes chemical weapons within the definition of WMDs.

Adds offenses involving biological weapons, chemical weapons, and nuclear materials to the racketeering predicate offense list.

(Sec. 6803) Provides criminal liability for participation in nuclear and WMD threats against the United States. Provides extraterritorial Federal jurisdiction over such offenses.

Subtitle J: Prevention of Terrorist Access to Destructive Weapons Act of 2004 – Prevention of Terrorist Access to Destructive Weapons Act of 2004 – (Sec. 6903) Amends the Federal criminal code to make it unlawful for any person to knowingly produce, construct (engineer or synthesize in the case of variola virus), otherwise acquire, transfer, receive, possess, import, export, or use, or possess and threaten to use: (1) missile systems designed to destroy aircraft; (2) radiological dispersal devices; or (3) variola virus.

Amends the Atomic Energy Act of 1954 to make it unlawful for any person to knowingly manufacture, produce, transfer, acquire, receive, possess, import, export, or use, or possess and threaten to use any atomic weapon.

Establishes penalties for such offenses including fines and imprisonment for 25 or 30 years to life.

Establishes Federal jurisdiction over such offenses where: (1) they occur in interstate or foreign commerce; (2) are committed by or against a U.S. national outside of the United States; (3) are committed against Federal property both within and outside of the United States; or (4) an offender aids or abets or conspires with any person over whom jurisdiction exists.

(Sec. 6907) Adds such offenses to: (1) the list of offenses for which orders authorizing the interception of wire, oral, or electronic communications may be obtained; (2) the definition of "Federal crime of terrorism" for purposes of provisions prohibiting acts of terrorism transcending international boundaries; and (3) the definition of "specified unlawful activity" for purposes of provisions addressing money laundering.

(Sec. 6910) Amends the Arms Export Control Act to add such offenses to the statutory list of adverse considerations supporting disapproval of an export license application.

Subtitle K: Pretrial Detention of Terrorists – Pretrial Detention of Terrorists Act of 2004 – (Sec. 6952) Creates a presumption of pretrial detention in certain cases involving terrorism.

Title VII: Implementation of 9/11 Commission Recommendations – 9/11 Commission Implementation Act of 2004 – **Subtitle A: Diplomacy, Foreign Aid, and the Military in the War on Terrorism** – (Sec. 7102) Makes findings and expresses the sense of Congress on U.S. policy on terrorist sanctuaries.

Amends the Export Administration Act of 1979 to extend restrictions on certain exports to countries whose territories are being used as sanctuaries for terrorists or terrorist organizations.

Amends the Foreign Relations Authorization Act, Fiscal Years 1988 and 1989 to require annual State Department country reports on terrorism to include detailed assessments with respect to each foreign country whose territory is being used as a sanctuary for terrorists or terrorist organizations. Specifies the required content of such reports, including: (1) how much knowledge foreign governments have as to terrorist activities in their countries; (2) actions by such countries to eliminate terrorist sanctuaries, cooperate with U.S. antiterrorism efforts, and prevent the proliferation of and trafficking in weapons of mass destruction (WMDs) in their countries; and (4) a strategy for addressing and eliminating terrorist sanctuaries.

(Sec. 7103) Expresses the sense of Congress with respect to U.S. commitment to the future of Pakistan. Extends through FY 2006 the authority of the President to waive certain foreign assistance restrictions on Pakistan.

(Sec. 7104) Afghanistan Freedom Support Act Amendments of 2004 – Expresses the sense of Congress that the U.S. Government should work with other countries to obtain long-term security, political, and financial commitments and fulfillment of pledges to the Government of Afghanistan.

Amends the Afghanistan Freedom Support Act of 2002 to require the President (under current law the President is "strongly urged") to designate within the State Department a coordinator of Afghanistan affairs. Requires the coordinator to submit to Congress the Administration's Afghanistan assistance plan and to coordinate the implementation of assistance to Afghanistan.

Reaffirms authorities in the Afghanistan Freedom Support Act of 2002 relating to economic and democratic development assistance for Afghanistan.

Requires the President to formulate a five-year strategy for Afghanistan and submit such strategy to Congress. Requires that such strategy include specific and measurable goals for addressing the long-term development and security needs of Afghanistan. Requires the President to submit annual report through 2010 on the progress in implementing such strategy.

Revises provisions relating to education, the rule of law, civil society and democracy, and protection of cultural sites in Afghanistan.

Directs the Secretary of State to submit periodic reports to Congress on assistance for Afghanistan from all U.S. Government agencies.

Declares it to be U.S. policy to: (1) take immediate steps to disarm private militias, particularly child soldiers, in Afghanistan; and (2) support the expansion of international peacekeeping and security operations in Afghanistan.

Expresses the sense of Congress supporting counterdrug efforts in Afghanistan. Directs the Secretaries of Defense and State to jointly report to Congress on: (1) the progress in reducing poppy cultivation and heroin production in Afghanistan; and (2) the use of profits from illegal drugs to support terrorist efforts to undermine the Government of Afghanistan.

Extends through January 1, 2010, the reporting requirement on the implementation of strategies for meeting the immediate and long-term security needs of Afghanistan.

Repeals provisions of the Foreign Assistance Act of 1961 prohibiting certain assistance to Afghanistan.

Authorizes appropriations through FY 2006 for assistance to Afghanistan.

(Sec. 7105) Expresses the sense of Congress with respect to the relationship between the peoples and Governments of the United States and Saudi Arabia.

(Sec. 7106) Expresses the sense of Congress on efforts to combat Islamist terrorism.

(Sec. 7107) Expresses the sense of Congress that U.S. foreign policy should promote democratic values and respect for the rule of law and that the U.S. Government must encourage all governments with predominantly Muslim populations to promote democratic values and respect for the rule of law.

(Sec. 7108) Expresses the sense of Congress with respect to the promotion of U.S. values through broadcast media.

Directs the Secretary of State to make grants to the National Endowment for Democracy to fund a private sector group to establish and manage a free and independent media network.

Authorizes appropriations.

(Sec. 7109) Amends the State Department Basic Authorities Act of 1956 to require the Secretary of State to: (1) make public diplomacy an integral component in the planning and execution of U.S. foreign policy; and (2) coordinate and develop a strategy for public diplomacy activities of Federal agencies.

Sets forth the duties of the Under Secretary of State for Public Diplomacy, including the preparation of an annual strategic plan for public diplomacy in collaboration and consultation with the regional and functional bureaus of the State Department.

(Sec. 7110) Declares U.S. policy on public diplomacy training. Directs the Secretary to: (1) emphasize the importance of public diplomacy in recruiting, training, and assigning members of the Foreign Service; and (2) seek to increase the number of Foreign Service officers who are proficient in languages spoken in predominantly Muslim countries. Makes proficiency in public diplomacy a criterion for promotion in the Foreign Service.

(Sec. 7111) Directs the President to continue to support and seek to expand the work of the democracy caucus at the United Nations General Assembly and the United Nations Human Rights Commission and to seek to establish a democracy caucus at the United Nations Conference on Disarmament and at other international organizations.

Directs the President to use the influence of the United States to reform criteria in United Nations bodies and other international organizations to exclude certain countries that violate the principles of specific organizations, are subject to United Nations sanctions, or have been determined to have supported international terrorism or terrorist organizations.

Declares U.S. policy supporting training courses in multilateral diplomacy for Foreign Service officers and other employees of the State Department. Directs the Secretary to provide training in multilateral diplomacy to Foreign Service officers and other employees of the State Department.

(Sec. 7112) Declares it to be U.S. policy that the United States should commit to a long-term engagement with Muslim populations, particularly with Muslim youth and those who influence youth. Expresses the sense of Congress that the United States should significantly increase its investment in programs which promote engagement with the Muslim world. Authorizes the President to substantially expand U.S. exchange, scholarship, and library programs, particularly programs that benefit Muslims.

Directs the Secretary to conduct a pilot program to make grants to U.S.-sponsored elementary and secondary schools in predominantly Muslim countries to provide full or partial merit-based scholarships to lower-income and middle-income families in such countries and to report to Congress on such program. Authorizes appropriations for FY 2005 and 2006.

(Sec. 7113) Authorizes the Secretary to establish an International Youth Opportunity Fund to provide financial assistance for the improvement of public education in the Middle East and other strategically-important countries with predominantly Muslim populations. Encourages the Secretary to seek the cooperation of the international community in establishing and supporting such Fund.

(Sec. 7114) Expresses the sense of Congress supporting the use of economic strategies to combat terrorism.

(Sec. 7115) Authorizes appropriations for FY 2005 and 2006 for the Middle East Partnership Initiative. Expresses the sense of Congress that a significant amount of such funding be made available to promote the rule of law in the Middle East.

(Sec. 7116) Expresses the sense of Congress that the President should engage foreign governments in developing a comprehensive multilateral strategy to fight terrorism. Authorizes the President to establish an international counterterrorism policy contact group with the leaders of foreign governments.

(Sec. 7117) Expresses the sense of Congress on the importance of targeting terrorist financial facilitators in the war on terrorism.

(Sec. 7118) Amends the Immigration and Nationality Act to revise procedures for the designation of foreign terrorist organizations. Provides for periodic review of the status of such organizations and the publication of such review in the Federal Register.

(Sec. 7119) Directs the President to submit to Congress a report on the activities of the U.S. Government to carry out the provisions of this subtitle, including descriptions of U.S. strategy to: (1) address and eliminate terrorist sanctuaries; (2) engage with Pakistan and support it over the long term; (3) engage with the Government of Saudi Arabia on subjects of mutual interest and importance; (4) help win the struggle of ideas in the Islamic world; (5) expand outreach to foreign Muslim audiences through broadcast media; (6) expedite issuance of visas to aliens for the purpose of participating in a scholarship, exchange, or visitor programs without compromising the security of the United States; (7) promote free universal basic education in the Middle East and in predominantly Muslim countries; and (8) encourage economic reform in predominantly Muslim countries.

(Sec. 7120) Amends the Case-Zablocki Act to require the Secretary of State to: (1) make publicly available on the State Department Internet website each treaty or international agreement to be published in the compilation entitled "United States Treaties and Other International Agreements" not later than 180 days after such treaty or agreement enters into force; and (2) submit to Congress an annual report containing an index of certain international agreements for the preceding calendar year.

Subtitle B: Terrorist Travel and Effective Screening – (Sec. 7201) Requires the Director of the National Counterterrorism Center to submit to Congress a strategy for combining terrorist travel intelligence, operations, and law enforcement into a cohesive effort to intercept terrorists, find terrorist travel facilitators, and constrain terrorist mobility.

Directs the Secretary, in conjunction with the Secretary of State, to submit to Congress a plan describing how the DHS and the Department of State (DOS) can acquire and deploy to all consulates, POEs, and immigration benefits offices technologies facilitating document authentication and the detection of potential terrorist indicators on travel documents.

Requires the Secretary, in coordination with the Secretary of State (as relevant to DOS personnel), to: (1) review and evaluate training programs regarding travel and identity documents, and techniques, patterns, and trends associated with terrorist travel provided to DHS and DOS personnel; and (2) implement related training and periodic retraining programs.

Directs the Secretary and the Secretary of State to individually submit annual reports on such training for their respective personnel.

Authorizes the Secretary to assist States, Indian tribes, local governments, and private organizations to establish training programs related to terrorist travel intelligence.

Requires the Director to increase resources and personnel to the small classified program that collects and analyzes intelligence on terrorist travel. Authorizes appropriations through FY 2009 for that purpose.

(Sec. 7202) Establishes a Human Smuggling and Trafficking Center, to be operated by the Secretary, the Secretary of State, and the Attorney General in accordance with their memorandum of understanding.

Requires the Center to: (1) serve as the focal point for interagency efforts to address terrorist travel; and (2) serve as a clearinghouse for Federal agency information in support of the U.S. strategy to prevent clandestine terrorist travel and the facilitation of migrant smuggling and trafficking of persons.

(Sec. 7203) Authorizes the Secretary of State to increase the number of consular officers by 150 per year through FY 2009.

Requires all immigrant and nonimmigrant visa applications to be reviewed and adjudicated by a consular officer (thus precluding the use of foreign nationals for visa screening).

Amends the Enhanced Border Security and Visa Entry Reform Act of 2002 to require consular officer training in document fraud detection.

Directs the Secretary of State, in coordination with the Secretary, to: (1) conduct a survey of each diplomatic and consular post at which visas are issued to assess the extent to which fraudulent documents are presented by visa applicants; and (2) not later than July 31, 2005, identify the posts experiencing the highest levels of fraud and place in each such post at least one full-time anti-fraud specialist unless a DHS employee with sufficient training and experience is already stationed there.

(Sec. 7204) Directs the President to seek the implementation of effective international measures to: (1) share information on lost, stolen, and fraudulent passports and other travel documents; (2) establish and implement a real-time verification system for such documents; and (3) encourage criminalization of certain conduct that could aid terrorist travel. Requires the President to submit annual progress reports on such efforts.

(Sec. 7205) Expresses the sense of Congress that the President should seek to enter into an international agreement to modernize and improve standards for the translation of names into the Roman alphabet in order to ensure common spellings for international travel documents and name-based watchlist systems.

(Sec. 7206) Requires the selection of at least 50 airports that lack pre-inspection stations for the current program of assigning additional immigration officers to assist air carriers in detecting fraudulent documents. Authorizes related appropriations through FY 2007.

(Sec. 7207) Requires the Secretary of State, no later than October 26, 2006, to certify which of the countries designated to participate in the visa waiver program are developing a program to issue machine readable, tamper-resistant visa documents that incorporate biometric identifiers.

(Sec. 7208) Requires the Secretary to: (1) develop a plan to accelerate full implementation of an automated biometric entry and exit data system (entry-exit system); (2) integrate the entry-exit system with all databases and data systems maintained by specified Federal agencies that process or contain information on aliens (including components of the DHS); (3) establish procedures to ensure the accuracy and integrity of data in the entry-exit system, including procedures for individuals to seek correction of such data; and (4) implement a registered traveler program to expedite processing of travelers entering and exiting the United States, which shall be integrated with the entry-exit system. Requires the standardization of information and data collected from foreign nationals as well as the procedures used to collect such data.

(Sec. 7209) Directs the Secretary, in consultation with the Secretary of State, to implement by January 1, 2008, a plan to require biometric passports or other secure passports for all travel into the United States by U.S. citizens and by categories of individuals for whom documentation requirements were previously waived.

(Sec. 7210) Expresses the sense of Congress that the U.S. Government should: (1) exchange terrorist information with trusted allies; (2) move toward real-time verification of passports with issuing authorities; (3) where practicable, conduct passenger prescreening for flights destined for the United States; (4) work with other countries to ensure effective airport inspection regimes; and (5) work with other countries to improve passport standards.

Requires the Secretary and the Secretary of State to submit a report on Federal efforts to collaborate with U.S. allies in the exchange of terrorist information.

Amends the Immigration and Nationality Act to require the Secretary to establish preinspection stations in at least 25 additional foreign airports. Requires the Secretary and the Secretary of State to submit a progress report on implementation of this requirement.

(Sec. 7211) Requires the Secretary of Health and Human Services (HHS) to establish minimum standards for birth certificates for use by Federal agencies for official purposes. Prohibits Federal agencies from accepting nonconforming birth certificates beginning two years after promulgation of such standards. Requires States to certify compliance with such standards.

Directs the Secretary of HHS to award grants to States to assist them in conforming to the minimum standards for birth certificates and in developing the capacity to match birth and death records.

(Sec. 7212) Requires the Secretary of Transportation to establish minimum standards for driver's licenses or personal identification cards issued by States for use by Federal agencies for identification purposes, following a negotiated rulemaking process that includes State representatives. Prohibits Federal agencies from accepting nonconforming driver's licenses or personal identification cards issued by a State more than two years after promulgation of such standards. Requires States to certify compliance with such standards.

Requires the Secretary of Transportation to award grants to States to assist them in conforming to such standards.

(Sec. 7213) Requires the Commissioner of Social Security to: (1) issue regulations restricting the issuance of multiple replacement social security cards; (2) establish minimum standards for the verification of records supporting an application for an original social security card; and (3) add death and fraud indicators to the social security number verification system.

Directs the Commissioner to establish an interagency task force for the improvement of social security cards and numbers. Requires the task force to establish security requirements.

Requires the Commissioner to: (1) make and report on specified improvements to the enumeration at birth program for the issuance of social security numbers to newborns; and (2) study and report on the most efficient options for ensuring the integrity of the process for enumeration at birth.

(Sec. 7214) Amends title II (Old-Age, Survivors and Disability Insurance) of the Social Security Act to prohibit the display of social security numbers on driver's licenses, motor vehicle registrations, or personal identification cards or the inclusion of such numbers in a magnetic strip, bar code, or other means of communication on such documents.

(Sec. 7215) Requires the Secretary to establish a program to oversee the implementation of DHS responsibilities with respect to terrorist travel, including the analysis, coordination, and dissemination of terrorist travel intelligence and operational information to specified DHS components and with other appropriate Federal agencies.

(Sec. 7216) Amends the Federal criminal code to increase penalties for fraud and related activity in connection with identification documents and information if committed to facilitate international terrorism.

(Sec. 7217) Directs the Secretary of State to study and report on the feasibility and benefits of establishing a system that provides border and visa issuance officials with real-time information on allegedly lost or stolen passports.

(Sec. 7218) Establishes a Visa and Passport Security Program within the DOS Bureau of Diplomatic Security.

(Sec. 7220) Requires the Secretary to propose minimum standards for identification documents required of domestic commercial airline passengers for boarding. States that such standards shall take effect when an approval resolution is passed by the House and Senate under specified procedures and becomes law.

Subtitle C: National Preparedness – (Sec. 7301) Expresses the sense of Congress supporting the adoption of a unified incident command system and the enhancement of communications connectivity between and among all levels of government and emergency response providers.

(Sec. 7302) Authorizes governmental entities in the National Capital Region (i.e., District of Columbia, Maryland, and Virginia) to enter into mutual aid agreements for emergency services in an emergency or public service event (e.g., undeclared emergency, presidential inauguration, public gatherings, etc.).

Limits the liability of first responders participating in mutual aid agreements.

(Sec. 7303) Directs the Secretary of Homeland Security to establish a program to enhance public safety interoperable communications at all levels of government. Authorizes the Secretary to establish an Office for Interoperability and Compatibility within the DHS Directorate of Science and Technology to carry out DHS programs relating to SAFECOM and other programs.

Authorizes appropriations.

Requires the Secretary to report to Congress on DHS plans for accelerating the development of national voluntary consensus standards for public safety interoperable communications.

Requires the President to coordinate cross-border interoperability issues between the United States, Mexico, and Canada.

Requires the Secretary to provide assistance to support the rapid establishment of consistent, secure, and effective interoperable communications capabilities in urban and high risk areas.

Authorizes the Secretary to make multiyear grants, up to three years, for enhancing interoperable communications capabilities for emergency response providers. Limits the amount for such grants to $150 million in any fiscal year. Requires grant applicants to submit an Interoperable Communications Plan to the Secretary for approval.

Requires the Office for Domestic Preparedness in DHS to assist State and local governments and emergency response providers to acquire interoperable communication technology.

Expresses the sense of Congress that interoperable emergency communications systems and radios should continue to be deployed for use by first responders, and that upgraded and new digital communications systems and new digital radios must meet prevailing standards for interoperability.

(Sec. 7304) Directs the Secretary to establish not fewer than two pilot projects in high threat urban areas or regions that are likely to implement a national model strategic plan to foster interagency communications and report to Congress on such pilot projects.

(Sec. 7305) Expresses the sense of Congress that DHS should promote adoption of voluntary national preparedness standards for the private sector.

(Sec. 7306) Requires the Secretary to report to Congress on the progress of DHS in completing vulnerability and risk assessments of the nation's critical infrastructure and the readiness of the U.S. Government to respond to threats.

(Sec. 7307) Expresses the sense of Congress that the Secretary of Defense should regularly assess the adequacy of the U.S. Northern Command's plans and strategies.

Subtitle D: Homeland Security – (Sec. 7401) Expresses the sense of Congress that Congress must pass legislation in the first session of the 109th Congress to reform the system for distributing grants to enhance State and local government prevention of, preparedness for, and response to acts of terrorism.

(Sec. 7402) Amends the Homeland Security Act of 2002 to include within the duties of the Special Assistant to the Secretary of Homeland Security: (1) the coordination of industry efforts to identify private sector resources and capabilities to supplement governmental efforts to prevent or respond to a terrorist attack; (2) the coordination with the Directorate of Border and Transportation Security and the Assistant Secretary for Trade Development of the Department of Commerce on issues related to the travel and tourism industries; and (3) consulting with the Office of State and Local Government Coordination and Preparedness on all matters of concern in the private sector, including the tourism industry.

(Sec. 7403) Directs the Secretary, in coordination with the Chairman of the Federal Communications Commission (FCC), to study the feasibility of establishing an emergency telephonic alert notification system and to report to Congress on such study.

(Sec. 7404) Directs the Secretary to conduct a pilot study for issuing public homeland security warnings using a system similar to the AMBER Alert communications network and to report to Congress on such study.

(Sec. 7405) Requires the Secretary to ensure that there is effective and ongoing coordination of Federal efforts to prevent, prepare for, and respond to acts of terrorism and other emergencies among the divisions of DHS.

(Sec. 7406) Amends the Robert T. Stafford Disaster Relief and Emergency Assistance Act to require the Director of the Federal Emergency Management Agency (FEMA) to establish a program of emergency preparedness compacts for acts of terrorism, disasters, and emergencies.

(Sec. 7407) Establishes in DHS the Office of Counternarcotics Enforcement. Sets forth the responsibilities of the Director of such Office for the control and interdiction of illegal drugs and the reporting requirements of such Office. Authorizes appropriations.

(Sec. 7408) Requires each subdivision of DHS that is a National Drug Control Program Agency to include in its employee performance appraisal system criteria relating to employee performance in the enforcement of narcotics laws.

Subtitle E: Public Safety Spectrum – (Sec. 7501) Expresses the sense of Congress that Congress must pass legislation in the first session of the 109th Congress that establishes a comprehensive approach to the timely return of analog broadcast spectrum as early as December 31, 2006, to permit public safety entities to begin using that spectrum.

(Sec. 7502) Requires certain studies and reports to Congress on allocations of spectrum for emergency response providers and strategies to meet public safety telecommunications requirements.

Subtitle F: Presidential Transition – Requires outgoing executive branch officials to provide the President-elect with a detailed classified, compartmented summary of specific threats to national security as soon as possible after the date of the general election.

Expresses the sense of the Senate that the Senate should give expedited consideration to national security officials nominated by a President-elect.

Provides for expedited security clearance determinations for members of a President-elect's transition team.

Subtitle G: Improving International Standards and Cooperation to Fight Terrorist Financing – (Sec. 7701) Expresses the sense of Congress that the Secretary of the Treasury should continue to promote the dissemination of international anti-money laundering and terrorist financing standards and to press for full implementation of the Financial Action Task Force recommendations to curb global terrorist financing.

(Sec. 7703) Amends the International Financial Institutions Act to require the Secretary to work with the International Monetary Fund (IMF) to combat terrorist financing and to testify before Congress on the status of implementation of international anti-money laundering and counter-terrorist financing standards by the IMF and other multilateral agencies.

(Sec. 7704) Directs the Secretary to continue to convene the interagency U.S. Government Financial Action Task Force working group to conduct annual reviews of anti-money laundering and counter-terrorist financing standards.

Subtitle H: Emergency Financial Preparedness – (Sec. 7801) Permits the Secretary of the Treasury to delegate the duties of the Fiscal Assistant Secretary to an employee of the Department of Treasury (current law restricts such delegation to an officer of the Treasury Department).

(Sec. 7802) Expresses the sense of Congress that the Secretary should educate consumers and employees of the financial services industry about domestic counterterrorist financing activities. Requires the Secretary to report to Congress on efforts to encourage a public-private partnership to protect critical financial infrastructure from terrorist attacks.

(Sec. 7803) Emergency Securities Response Act of 2004 – Amends the Securities Exchange Act of 1934 to expand the authority of the Securities and Exchange Commission (SEC) to issue orders or take other actions to protect investors and markets in emergency situations. Grants similar reciprocal authority to the Secretary of the Treasury in emergency situations.

Requires the Board of Governors of the Federal Reserve System, the Comptroller of the Currency, and the SEC to submit to Congress a joint report by April 30, 2006, on the efforts of the private sector to implement the Interagency Paper on Sound Practices to Strengthen the Resilience of the U.S. Financial System.

(Sec. 7804) Expresses the sense of Congress that the insurance industry and credit-rating agencies should consider a company's compliance with standards for private sector disaster and emergency preparedness in assessing insurability and creditworthiness.

Title VIII: Other Matters – Subtitle A: Intelligence Matters – Requires the Director of National Intelligence to establish a formal relationship, including information sharing, between the elements of the intelligence community and the National Infrastructure Simulation and Analysis Center.

Subtitle B: Department of Homeland Security Matters – (Sec. 8201) Establishes the Office of Geospatial Management within the DHS Office of the Chief Information Officer to coordinate DHS geospatial information needs (e.g., maps, charts, remote sensing data, and aerial photography). Authorizes appropriations.

Subtitle C: Homeland Security Civil Rights and Civil Liberties Protection – Homeland Security Civil Rights and Civil Liberties Protection Act of 2004 – (Sec. 8302) Amends the Homeland Security Act of 2002 to requires DHS, as part of its agency mission, to ensure that the civil rights and civil liberties of persons are not diminished by the efforts, activities, and programs aimed at securing the homeland.

(Sec. 8303) Expands the duties of the Officer for Civil Rights and Civil Liberties in DHS to include compliance and investigative responsibilities.

(Sec. 8304) Directs the Inspector General of DHS to designate a senior official for the protection of civil rights and liberties against abuses by DHS employees and contractors.

(Sec. 8305) Requires the DHS Privacy Officer to coordinate with the Officer for Civil Rights and Liberties in implementing DHS privacy programs, policies, and procedures.

(Sec. 8306) Requires the Secretary to ensure that DHS complies with protections for human research subjects.

Subtitle D: Other Matters – (Sec. 8401) Amends the Clinger-Cohen Act to require increased security for information technology capital planning and investment control responsibilities.

(Sec. 8402) Requires the FBI to continually maintain and update an enterprise architecture. Defines "enterprise architecture" as a detailed outline or blueprint of the information technology of the FBI. Requires the Director of the FBI to report to the House and Senate Judiciary Committees on whether the major information technology investments of the FBI are in compliance with the agency's enterprise architecture.

(Sec. 8403) Requires the Office of Government Ethics to submit to Congress a report evaluating the financial disclosure process for executive branch employees.

Requires the Office of Personnel Management to transmit to major party presidential nominees an electronic record on presidentially appointed positions.

Requires the head of each Federal agency to submit to the President and Congress a presidential appointment reduction plan.

Requires the Office of Government Ethics to conduct a comprehensive review of conflict of interest laws relating to executive branch employment and report to the President and Congress on such review.

(Sec. 8404) Amends the Aviation and Transportation Security Act to extend until November 19, 2005, provisions requiring air carriers to honor tickets issued by airlines that have suspended passenger service.

APPENDIX F
Foreign Intelligence Surveillance Act of 1978

50 U.S.C. §§ 1801–1811, 1821–1829, 1841–1846, 1861–1862, 1871.

BACKGROUND

Like Title III of the Omnibus Crime Control and Safe Streets Act of 1968 (the "Wiretap Act"), the Foreign Intelligence Surveillance Act (FISA) legislation was the result of congressional investigations into Federal surveillance activities conducted in the name of national security. Through FISA Congress sought to provide judicial and congressional oversight of foreign intelligence surveillance activities while maintaining the secrecy necessary to effectively monitor national security threats. FISA was initially enacted in 1978 and sets out procedures for physical and electronic surveillance and collection of foreign intelligence information. Initially FISA addressed only electronic surveillance but has been significantly amended to address the use of pen registers and trap and trace devices, physical searches and business records.

FISA also established the United States Foreign Intelligence Surveillance Court (FISC), a special U.S. Federal court that holds nonpublic sessions to consider issuing search warrants under FISA. Proceedings before the FISC are ex parte, meaning the government is the only party present.

GENERAL PROVISIONS

FISA, as amended, establishes procedures for the authorization of electronic surveillance, use of pen registers and trap and trace devices, physical searches and business records for the purpose of gathering foreign intelligence.

Electronic Surveillance Procedures – Subchapter I of FISA – established procedures for the conduct of foreign intelligence surveillance and created the FISC. The Department of Justice must apply to the FISC to obtain a warrant authorizing electronic surveillance of foreign agents. For targets that are U.S. persons (U.S. citizens, permanent resident aliens, and U.S. corporations), FISA requires heightened requirements in some instances.

- Unlike domestic criminal surveillance warrants issued under Title III of the Omnibus Crime Control and Safe Streets Act of 1968 (the "Wiretap Act"), agents need to demonstrate probable cause to believe that the "target of the surveillance is a foreign power or agent of a foreign power," that "a significant purpose" of the surveillance is to obtain "foreign intelligence information" and that appropriate "minimization procedures" are in place. 50 U.S.C. § 1804.
- Agents do not need to demonstrate that commission of a crime is imminent.
- For purposes of FISA, agents of foreign powers include agents of foreign political organizations and groups engaged in international terrorism, as well as agents of foreign nations. 50 U.S.C. § 1801.

Record Destruction: Where the government has accidentally intercepted communications that "under circumstances in which a person has a reasonable expectation of privacy and a warrant would be required for law enforcement purposes, and if both the sender and all intended recipients are located within the United States," the government is required to destroy those records, "unless the Attorney General determines that the contents indicate a threat of death or serious bodily harm to any person." 50 U.S.C. § 1806.

Exception to Court Order Requirement: The President may authorize electronic surveillance to acquire foreign intelligence information for periods of up to one year without a FISC court order where the Attorney General certifies that there is "no substantial likelihood that the surveillance will acquire the contents of any communication to which a U.S. person is a party," provided the surveillance is directed solely at communications among or between foreign powers, or "the acquisition of technical intelligence … from property or premises under the open and exclusive control of a foreign power." 50 U.S.C. § 1802.

Physical Searches – Subchapter II of FISA – establishes procedures for the physical search of "premises or property … owned, used, possessed by, or... in transit to or from a foreign power or an agent of a foreign power." The procedures are substantially similar to the procedures established for electronic foreign intelligence surveillance.

Pen Registers and Trap & Trace Devices for Foreign Intelligence Purposes – Subchapter III of FISA – establishes procedures for the use of pen registers and trap and trace devices for conducting telephone or e-mail surveillance.

Access to Certain Business Records for Foreign Intelligence Purposes – Subchapter IV of FISA – establishes procedures for obtaining a FISC order for third-party production of business records to acquire foreign intelligence information.

AMENDMENTS

FISA has been significantly amended by the Intelligence Authorization Act of 1995 (Pub. L. 103–359; 10/14/94) by the Intelligence Authorization Act of 1999 (Pub. L. 105–272; 10/5/98), by the USA PATRIOT Act (Pub. L. 107–156; 10/26/01), by the USA PATRIOT Additional Reauthorization Amendments Act of 2006 (Pub. L. 109–178; (3/9/06), the FISA (Foreign Intelligence Surveillance Act) Amendments Act of 2008 (Pub. L.110–261; 7/10/2008) and by the FISA Sunsets Extension Act (Pub. L. 112–113; 2/25/11). It also "eas[ed] the restrictions on foreign intelligence gathering within the United States and afford[ed] the U.S. intelligence community greater access to information unearthed during a criminal investigation." CRS Report RS21203, USA PATRIOT Act: A Sketch. Also see the other analyses of the PATRIOT Act for more on FISA changes as the result of passage of the PATRIOT Act. The FISA Amendments Act of 2008 also amended the ECPA.

CIVIL RIGHTS AND CIVIL LIBERTIES IMPLICATIONS

FISA prohibits surveillance of or production of business records regarding a U.S. person based solely on First Amendment activities. 50 U.S.C. §§ 1805, 1842, 1861. Section 1806 provides guidance on the sharing of foreign intelligence information among Federal agencies and with State and local partners, as well as guidance as to disclosure of foreign intelligence information in criminal proceedings. Section 1825 provides similar guidance regarding the use and disclosure of foreign intelligence gathered via a physical search, while section 1845 provides similar guidance for the use and disclosure of information acquired through pen registers and trap and trace devices gathered under Subchapter III. Note that "agents of foreign powers" may include U.S. citizens and permanent residents suspected of being engaged in espionage and violating U.S. law on territory under United States control. Section 1801(b).

The Intelligence Reform and Terrorism Prevention Act of 2004, P.L. 108–458, amended the definition of "agent of a foreign power" in FISA (50 U.S.C. § 1801(b)(1)), to add a new category of covered individuals called the "lone wolf" provision. Under the "lone wolf" provision a non-United States person who engages in international terrorism or activities in preparation for international terrorism is deemed to be an "agent of a foreign power" under FISA.

Wittes, Benjamin. 2011. What Benjamin Franklin Really said, *Hoover Institute*. http://www. Hoover.org/research/what-benjamin-franklin-really-said.

Social and Legal Challenges to Intelligence Collection

After the intelligence failures to predict and prevent the attacks on 9/11 twenty years ago and based on the findings of the 9/11 Commission Report both the federal law enforcement and intelligence community were reorganized (9/11 Commission, 2004). The challenge to the intelligence community in part based on that report was to enhance intelligence collection.

1. One of several areas where intelligence collection was increased was by means of singles intelligence. This involved the interception of phone and internet communications to include those communications of citizens of the United States in violation of the United States Constitution and federal law. This situation created not only a social backlash against the intelligence community but legal challenges as well (Goldman, 2006). While it is important to collect intelligence the right of the citizens cannot be violated and the United States Constitution and federal law must be followed. Some would say that it is worth giving up rights to prevent terrorism. As stated by Benjamin Franklin, "Those who would give of essential Liberty, to pursue a little temporary Safety, deserver neither Liberty or Safety." The statement by Benjamin Franklin in a 1775 letter was focusing on funding for the nation, which is an excellent statement that can be applied to this situation (Witter, 2011).

REFERENCES

9/11 Commission. 2004. *The 9/11 Commission Report*. New York: W.W. Norton & Company.

Dulles, Allen. 1963. *The Craft of Intelligence*. New York: Harper & Row.

Goldman, Jan. 2006. *Ethics of Spying: A Reader for the Intelligence Professional*. Lanham:Scarecrow Press.

Lowenthal, Mark and Clark, Robert. 2016. *The 5 Disciplines of Intelligence Collection*. NewYork: SAGE.

Wittes, Benjamin, 2011. What Benjamin Franklin Really Said. *Hoover Institute*. Retrieved from http://www.Hover.org/research/what-benjamin-franklin-really-said

Traditional Methods

Open-source intelligence has been an effective source of intelligence for many years. In the past it was obtained from newspapers, news cast on TV and radio, professional publications, company and government publications, conference and just talking to individuals who work at a targeted location. All of those methods are still utilized for open-source intelligence. All of this information can be obtained as no risk to the one collecting the information. It has always been a source of intelligence. What is recent is the internet and social media as a source of ONSINT. Before those platforms there has always been newspaper, journals, books, conferences and just people talk about things they should not in bars and public places. The phrase from World War II "Lose Lips Sink Ships," open-source intelligence (New Hampshire Government, 2020). Even Sherlock Holmes in the 1980s used the London Times and papers of the time for open-source information (Doyle, 1883).

The issue of reliability of OSINT is key as you mentioned in your post. As with all types of intelligence that is collected there needs to be the ability to verify the information received. This can be accomplished by using several sources. The various sources are then cross referenced to determine how accurate it is. Open source can be used as disinformation by an adversary as well (Clark, 2013).

REFERENCES

Clark, Robert. 2013. *Intelligence Analysis: A Target-Centric Approach*. Washington DC: Sage.

Doyle, A.C. 1883. *The Adventures of the Naval Treaty.* London: *The Strand Magazine.*
New Hampshire Government. 2020. World War II Posters at the State Library.
    Retrieved from https://www.nh.gov/nhsl/ww2/loose.html

Internet

In recent years open-source intelligence can now be obtained from the global communication found on the internet. All one needs to do is type in what type of information one is seeking and copious amount of data will appear. Using the internet one can also search company and government web sites. These are excellent sources containing a wealth of open-source intelligence that can be obtained not only of the specific information sought but also background information that is related to the search topic. All of this information can be obtained as no risk to the one collecting the information.

Social Media

Social media platforms such as Facebook, Twitter and others are another excellent method to obtain open-source intelligence. The information obtained can be very specific to individuals' communications on such platforms and can be a method to obtain critical information and a means to begin a dialog with the individuals in order to recruit such individuals for human intelligence. For the most part information can be obtained as no risk to the one collecting the information (Weggemans, 2013).

Challenges

Challenges associated with open-source information include the reliability of the information. The bias that may be imbedded in the information. Information that is presented in open sources as purposeful misinformation. Privacy issues and public relations.

The reliability of the information.

Just because information is available on the internet, social media, in publications, on television and in a conservation does not mean that it is accurate and reliable information. There may be errors or omission in the content that does not provide an accurate or complete representation of the facts related to the information obtained (Lowenthal & Clark, 2016).

The information obtained in this manner and from these sources need to be cross referenced with other sources in an attempt to determine the accuracy of the information.

The bias that may be imbedded in the information.

Information that is obtained from the internet, social media, in publications, on television and in a conservation in many situations could reflect the bias of the individual or individuals presenting the information in these forums. People do have bias and it is often reflected in information that they provide. The information obtained from these sources need to be cross referenced with other sources in an attempt to determine the accuracy of the information.

Information that is presented in open sources as purposeful misinformation.

One needs to be alert of the fact that information obtained from open sources has been planted as misinformation (Hoover, 1958). This could be done by individual, companies or adversary intelligence services. As always the information obtained from these sources must be cross referenced with other sources in an attempt to determine the accuracy of the information.

Privacy issues and public relations.

The collection of open-source intelligence on social media and especially from individual social media accounts by the intelligence community may be a legal privacy issue but assuredly can be publication relations privacy issue with the public. Even if legal many in the public will not be receptive to the intelligence-community-obtained information in this manner. It is vital for the intelligence community to know what is and is not legal to ensure that right are not violated and to avoid intelligence oversight investigations (Lowenthal & Clark, 2016).

Future

As global communications on all of these various open-source platforms continue to expand in the future challenges of accuracy, bias, misinformation as well as privacy and public relations it will continue to be a challenge for the intelligence community. In the furniture the intelligence community must review the open-source information obtained to guard against the flaws in the information obtained. If abuses by the intelligence community occur or are perceived by the public or Congress, it may lead to legal restrictions against the intelligence community as well as civil and criminal actions.

INDEX

Note: *Italic* page numbers refer to figures.

Foreign Intelligence Surveillance
Court (FISA) 11
Foreign Relations Authorization
Act 182
Forest Laboratories, Inc. v. Pillsbury Co.,
452 F.2d 621 (CA7, 1971) 119
Franklin, Benjamin 198
Freedom of Information Act 130
French Intelligence Community 47
French Resistance forces 3, 4
Future Years Defense Program 150

Galtieri, Leopoldo 74
General Provisions 174–175
geospatial intelligence 64
German Intelligence Community
46–47
German-occupied Europe 4, 5
Government Code and Cypher
School 43
Government Communications
Headquarters 43
government organizations 56
Grand Jury Information Sharing 179
Grey data 57

Hall, Virginia 3–4
Harbor Maintenance Trust Fund 162
Hazard Information System of the
National Oceanic and
Atmospheric Administration
143
Highway Trust Fund 162
Homeland Security Act 2002 9–10,
31, 191–192, 193; Airline
War Risk Insurance
Legislation 156–157; Arming
Pilots Against Terrorism
160–162; Conforming and
Technical Amendments
163; Coordination With
Non- Federal Entities
146–154; Corrections to
Existing Law Relating to
Airline Transportation

Security 162–163; Critical
Infrastructure Information
Act 2002 129–130; Department
of Homeland Security 127–
128; Department of Justice
Divisions 154–156; Directorate
of Border and Transportation
Security 136–143; Emergency
Preparedness and Response
143–145; Federal Workforce
Improvement 157–159;
information analysis and
infrastructure protection
128–129; Information Security
130–131; Office of Science
and Technology 131–132;
Science and Technology
in Support of Homeland
Security 132–136; Secretary
for Management 145–146;
Transition 162; Treatment
of Charitable Trusts for
Members of the Armed
Forces of the United States
and Other Governmental
Organizations 145
Homeland Security Advanced
Research Projects Agency 134
Homeland Security Civil Rights and
Civil Liberties Protection
193–194
Homeland Security Council 25
Homeland Security Information
Sharing Act 152
Homeland Security Science and
Technology Advisory
Committee 136
Hoover, J. Edgar 29
Hopper Information Services
Center 35
hostile nations, threats from 6,
7; Islamic Emirate of
Afghanistan 13, 16; Islamic
Republic of Iran 13, 16;
People's Democratic Republic

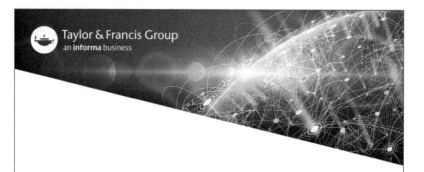